JustUs Behind Lies

Kimberly Fields

This is a work of nonfiction. It reflects the author's present recollection of experiences. Some names and identifying details have been changed to protect the privacy of individuals. No characters have been invented, no event or locations has fabricated and some dialogue has been recreated.

Justus Behind Lies: a novella / Kimberly Fields

Unbounded Creations Publishing House

Paperback Original

ISBN- 978-0-692-98852-7

www.kimberlyafields.com
womenalty@gmail.com

DEDICATION

To my honey bunches of oats, you sacrificed your life,
you gave your all, you stepped in when others walked out and
while you were away you—still provided. For that I thank
you!
I Love You.

My three Princes, the last several years have been a major
change for you all. And I understand the hurt, anger and
frustration you guys may have within. I apologize and
promise things will only get better now that this chapter is
over!
J.V., A.V., & J.F

ACKNOWLEDGMENTS

I wish to personally thank those who played a part in my husband's life during the period that led up to his arrest and afterwards, for your actions are what led to my inspiration and knowledge in creating this story.

My dear readers. Thank you once again for picking up my work of art. With so many wonderful authors out here. I am truly grateful you chose me.

~I am Kimberly A Fields.

~JAMES EARL~

James drove his sparkling pastel blue 1967 Cutlass convertible with shiny chrome rims through south Minneapolis, the hood that was known as the Bloods territory, once his homeboys until the green-eyed monster separated them. James, who went by James Earl, was all about money; them niggas were about nothing less than the gutters they were from. Cruising with James was his homie, Black, another reason why the Bloods had hate for him. They rode high like two Roman emperors in their chariot, slowly checking out the babes strolling on the sidewalk. James let his left arm rest on the door; his right arm stretched straight over the wheel, as he looked to his right and suddenly flared up. He smacked Black. "Stop that."

"Wat up?" Black yelled in a high-pitched voice.

"Watch where you put your dirt, you nasty nigga!" Black looked at some tobacco flakes falling out of his jeans' pocket. Black was lanky and tall, about six foot four, towering over James, but feared the smaller man. James, being the sparrow that he was, was high yellow, curly hair, standing at only five foot eight, a pretty nigga, mouth full of gold and a pocket full of cash. James knew the unwritten code of the streets, and few challenged him. Black brushed the tobacco off the seat. Smack. James clipped the side of Black's head. If there was anything he loved more than his life, it was his cars. Like most black men, James proved his worth by putting every dollar in his rides.

"Aww man!" Black had had enough. "What is wrong with you? It's…"

It was about then that an all too familiar sound altered the conversation and Black ducked down low, crouching as best he could into the tight space between the seat and the glove compartment. If he could, Black tried to squeeze under the dashboard. James slammed the gas pedal, and the Cutlass careened and skidded as James made his getaway. There were three or four loud pops. James would later find two bullet holes on the side of his precious blue classic. That was unacceptable. His nostrils widened, and his eyes squinted into black pearls as he entered a zone of rage. You could say this is where it all started, yet James didn't know who shot at him. But he knew it was the Bloods. This was the beginning of the war between the two. Dating one of them didn't help nor make it better. They hated him! Why? No one knew. The fact that James was all about his money could have been the only reason. Some envied him, while others would do anything to see him flat on his ass. Having a nefarious woman for a mother who remarried and brought James to Minneapolis, just like every rebellious teenager who comes from a broken home, the streets were soon to become his family, and violence in this Midwestern city during the 1990s had given Minneapolis, MN the name Murderapolis. Where did James get all that anger? It could have been a lot of reasons, but he snapped when he saw his Cutlass.

Months earlier James had an altercation with Edward, which involved Black and Chris. Edward was one of the Bloods. In fact, he was the relative of the Bloods gang leader as well as one of James' girlfriend's cousins. Waiting on Black and Chris to arrive at his mom's house, James grabbed a 9mm gun from under his bed, sticking it in the small of his back. He had no problems squaring up with a nigga. But just in case a bitch ass nigga wanted to fight dirty…

The three of them hopped in James' Cutlass and began to roam the hood. While riding down 4th Avenue, Chris spotted Edward standing outside one of the Bloods' aunt's house. James pulled up, and Chris challenged Edward to a fight. Edward approached the car but turned and ran when he saw that Black, sitting in the front seat, had a gun. Edward dashed between houses on 4th Avenue, leading to Clinton Avenue south. James sped around the corner, hoping to catch him; yet Edward had disappeared. James broke fast and headed to his girl's house, dropping Chris and Black off on the way, and then making a pit stop at a stash house. James had to make a trip out of town that night, so he had to get some things in order.

Later that night, everyone staggered out of the Legend into the crisp cold air, looking to see who they were linking up with tonight, chicks half dressed and full of that liquid poison. Black walked out chopping it up with some young yam. Since James took off, he decided to kick some breeze and cool it that night. After getting the yam's number, Black drove down 3rd Avenue. He spotted Edward standing on the corner of 33rd and 3rd Avenue with some dude. From the looks of their demeanor and hand movement, he could tell they were arguing. Dude was tall, slim and dark-skinned, white t-shirt and red chucks—from the looks of his attire he had to be one of the Bloods. The conversation was getting heated. He sat back and watched for a minute. Edward was getting frustrated, moving back and forth in place. He must have got fed up, because he walked off.

"Yeah, I got you, nigga! "Black expressed. His eyes were squinted, lips turned upside down, nose flared, face twisted, as he could already smell the stench of Edward's death. He hit the block hoping Edward was heading home. Pulling up to the lights on 38th Street, Black parked at the corner on 39th and 4th Avenue. Assuming Edward was going straight home, he drove ahead and parked. He sauntered in the dark air, quietly taking a step, then pausing, heading in the direction of Edward's house; on the lot of the house he crept low and hid behind a tree and sat down on the grass, resting his back against the tree trunk. It was dark and late; half the city was asleep, and the other half drugged out. He didn't care because he was getting him. He sat two houses down, waiting and wishing this nigga would hurry up. The next twenty minutes seemed like hours.

Black's pager began to vibrate, and the code 69 popped up. There was a change of plans for Black. He then saw Edward turn the corner, walking with what more than likely was his girl. Black jumped up, marching across the lawns, with his nine locked and loaded, hands gripped tightly as he held his arms horizontally. The two were in deep conversation. Black started walking. Just as he got to the bushes by the house, a shadow appeared out of nowhere. Edward stepped into the fire. BAM–BAM–BAM. Shots rang, and crisp bangs grabbed the night's attention with the authority of death. His bitch screamed wildly, yelling out for her Edward, who writhed in hollow, soul piercing deep moans.

Lurking in the shadows, holding two pepperoni pizzas in a warmer, was a pizza deliveryman. Shaking, he nearly whimpered from fright, but instead lost control and peed in his pants. Black was surprised; it was the dude from the club. Black dashed back through the houses. The shooter ran across the street through the houses, passing the pizza man, and disappeared into the night without evening seeing him. The pizza man jumped into his car and sped off.

Edward lost a leg below the knee and suffered massive blood loss from the gunshot, which literally tore most of his right leg in half, nearly severing a major artery to the point he could have died. But the medical team quickly saved his life. It was at the hospital when Edward told the doctors and nurses his assailant was James, although he knew the shooter was at least six feet something and dark, very dark-skinned. He told the detectives he was shot at with a nine-millimeter handgun.

Days later, the neighborhood saw two suits knocking on doors. It was not hard to know who they were because one of them was a lanky white guy. The only white people to go door-to-door were either people from the suburbs or trendy urban condos who believed in reform and represented political candidates, who themselves would rarely be seen in such neighborhoods. Maybe an occasional salesperson, but that was rarer in the 90s than it used to be. Now, everyone could see who these dudes were in their cheap suits from JC Penney.

One was tall, maybe six foot three, and had a big brownish-red mustache, slightly fluffy and needing a trim. Perhaps that is why they called him Fluffy down at the station. He was a good cop, trying to do what was right. When he entered the academy, it was all about helping society. Now, it was more or less doing the work. But this one was different. The kid had a hole blown through his lower leg, leaving it amputated. The city was more violent than just five years before, and the department wanted to make a statement. Detective Steven Reid knew the case had to be solved quickly. Reid was a veteran of nearly 13 years, and at age 35, he had both a hatred of the streets and a sense that not everything was as it appeared. Not every young black kid was an ignorant thug set out to rip you off, or at least Reid did not believe they were born that way.

Detective Jerome Johnson, or Jay-Jay, as he was called, was on assignment with Reid to crack this case. At just shy of six feet, Jay-Jay appeared short next to Reid but had a stronger frame. Dark-skinned, Jay-Jay was a handsome man who had done everything right. At the age of sixteen he went to a mentorship program for wayward kids, or at-risk youth, as some like to say. Jay-Jay was still relatively new to the force at only 23 years of age, but seasoned to the street life, mostly because his roots were in this exact area. Reid was tired of all the nonsense, as he called it. These thugs were thugs, and he knew exactly what their intentions were and felt they were animals at best. Lock them up and heck, maybe if one of them gets a bit out of line, save some money and avoid the jail time. Yes, a bit extreme, and some of Jay-Jay's black friends felt he was a traitor. But to Jay-Jay it was not about race—it was about the streets.

The two worked hard, knowing that games had to be played. No one would snitch in a place like this. After all, who would protect them after the cops made an arrest? It was not only a dangerous world; it was a completely different world from what a lot of your "average" Americans could even fathom. Tell what you know to the cops? Are you kidding me? You saw what happened to Edward. So Reid and Johnson played the roles of Good Cop and Bad Cop, and yet somehow, the two knew their audience had witnessed this movie before. No one was fooled. An elderly man did remember hearing a car tear out of there so fast it left a year of rubber on the road. At least that is how the old man phrased it, yet he was just happy to have the attention of the two suits—comfortable enough to mention that, but nothing more. They started to question if the man had even seen a car.

A week or so before the shooting, there was another shooting in the neighborhood directed at a Ford Thunderbird convertible. Rumor on the street was that the nineteen-year-old driving the car knew some gang members and may have been one himself. That teen was James, the wrong kid at the wrong place with anger issues. Seemed like a closed case. The department didn't want to spend more time than necessary and certainly no more dollars than they should.

Reid pounded on James mother's door.

"What do you want?" a stout, short black woman hollered through the door.

"Ms. Harris?"

"Like I said, what do you want?" the woman barked through the locked door.

"Ma'am, this is the police…"

"I can tell that. I asked you what is it that you want?" The woman's voice grew raspy and louder, clearly at a breaking point. She opened the inner door but kept the screen door locked as a barrier between her and these intruders who no one wanted on their block.

"Ms. Harris, is your son at home?"

"Who?"

Reid placed his palm flat against Jay-Jay right arm and brushed him aside. This was not the time for games. "Ma'am, now listen to me real careful." He waved his badge across her face as he stared at her, gluing on his meanest gang face he could find from his youth and shot at her, "This is about attempted homicide, lady, this isn't a joke."

The woman's feet danced a step back, and she appeared disarranged. Maybe a little dizzy. She looked at the two men. "It depends on who you looking for. Mine ain't here, but I'll tell them you stopped by." Ms. Harris closed the door.

Four days later James was back. He got word that some detectives wanted to talk with him about the shooting regarding Edward. He was cool about it; he didn't do it, and he wasn't here. But could he prove it? Remember the man in the shadows of the trees that had seen everything? The pizza deliveryman spoke with the police. He told how he had seen a black man lurking, being about six feet, and he also noticed the shotgun. He had seen everything, even the man's discolored face. And so did Black; he was there too, no mistaking it, but it was James they wanted, based on Edward's statement.

The trial did not take long, and James' attorney was a public defender who seemed more concerned with getting home to watch TV than with proving that his client was innocent. He probably did not feel it was worth his time.

Edward testified hearing a gun cock, and he saw Darnell (Black) Young. That's when he told his girlfriend to run, and then he began to run. He believed he heard seven shots fired, that Darnell (Black) Young was wearing black and that people

11

other than Young were also present. He testified that he saw James Fields run up to him and try to shoot him in the head, but stated that he blocked the shot with his arm and played dead, then saw Fields turn to Young and say, "I got him."

However, Edward's girlfriend testified that she heard only two shots and that Young was wearing a white shirt and khaki pants. The eyewitness saw just one person with a shotgun and heard two shots. A woman who lived upstairs from Edward Evans' aunt testified she heard two shots and based on forensics reports; there were two shell cases found from a sawed-off shotgun.

Edward lost a leg below the knee. One-leg Edward, as he became known by, was the center of the attempted murder trial. A year later is when the courts found James guilty, sentencing him to 180 months. Following right behind him was Black, who was soon to join him, but with a lesser charge of an accomplice to attempted murder. Who would have thought one little altercation would rob a man of 15 years of his life based on lies, hate, and poor investigation? And soon again, JustUs Behind Lies would be served.

~Winter Release~

Walking out the metal doors of Oak Park Heights. As a partial free man, James inhaled the cold crisp October air. Having six hours to report to the halfway house, with a smile as bright as the shining sun, James joyfully walk up to the car of his girlfriend's. While locked up, there were a few broads he kept in touch with. But it was Toni who happen to have things together for his release. She was financially stable and had her own crib. Not that he needed her for money. But knowing that she could stand on her own made him more attracted to her. After 15 years of eating garbage. The first stop they made was to McDonald's. Then did a quick round to family members houses and to see his kids. Finally, making it to the Southside of Minneapolis, James checked into the workhouse.

On a mission to get his life back on track, it wasn't long before he was employed with a metal molding company. For an ex-hustler, the income was fair, and it allowed him to keep a comfortable lifestyle. See, this time around would be different. There was no way he was trying to go back to that hellhole. Looking forward to making up lost time with his children. James was prepared to live a law bidden life.

January 2008, he moved out of the halfway house and in with his girlfriend Toni. For things to be good on his end, the landlord had to give the okay that a convicted tempted murderer could stay at the property. As far as he was concerned, everything was good. So, in this four—bedroom townhome, James, Toni and her daughter lived there. At times her other children would visit on a regular basis. It got to the point where they just moved in.

"This shit too much." James sat thinking about how he was now taking care of a household with not only his girl but also her grown kids and their children. The amount of traffic that was coming and going made the landlord suspicious. While out of town vising his mother, the landlord called Toni questioning why there was a truck belonging to a convicted murderer parked in the driveway. That's when she exposed that she lied about getting approval for James to be there. The fact that she risked his freedom so he could be with her

was the first sign that their relationship wasn't going to work.

Making sure his parole officer didn't find out about the issue she created. James had Toni find him a place to live. Searching the north side, she found a three—bedroom, two—bathroom house on 40th and Russell. Both signing the lease; Toni kept her place where she remained. Things were good for several months; he was working, building a relationship with his children, and staying out of trouble. But James wasn't prepared for the chaos he was about to walk into. Arriving to work on time, as he parked his car, he could see a crowd of co—workers standing with signs. The company was on strike. For a full week, he went in, praying things would change. That employees would come to some terms with the human service department. By the second week of the strike, the company started to lay off folks. He wasn't trying to rely on Toni. Feeling his back against the wall, knowing he could have looked for another job. Instead, he would soon find his way to what he knew best. Knowing he had bills to keep up with, James gave in. Emptying out his locker, he walked out the building for the last time. Walking to his car, one of James co—workers ran up to him. As the guy begin to talk, James couldn't help but laugh. Every syllable that came out was in Spanish. "Naw, Naw bruh. I don't speak Spanish—I'm black." So many people confuse him for being Mexican.

"Oh, sorry holmes, I thought you were Mexican."

"So many people confuse me for being Mexican—but what's good?

"I came to see what you got going on as a backup? I mean you being released from prison and all. I know you gone need some dinero Holmes"

"Man, I'm trying to figure that out. Why, what you got going on?"

"I got that pure blanco."

"Word?"

***

Stopping at Toni's place to change clothes. Toni became hostel, curious to where he was about to go and with whom. She ask where he was going, as he gathers all his things. James ignored her—he had no intentions of coming back. With what he was about to get into, he needed privacy.

A few weeks later, James took all he had out the bank and put it on the line. Hooking up with the Mexican—after a month he made back triple. He knew he would need help to make the moves he was about to take. Leaving Toni's spot, he hit up Black to meet him at Maxwell's Pub. He found Black sitting at a table in the far back. Getting right to business, James shared what he came across. They threw back a few and chopped it up a little more. From the first bid and doing time behind Black, it probably wasn't a good idea to be getting dirty with him. But that was his brother and James just knew he had his back. Plus, he needed more help with the amount he had moved in just one week. The decision to turn his life around went out the window. After having a few with Black, he wasn't ready to go in for the night. He hit up his old co—worker Dino and they decided to meet up and Augies Strip Club downtown Minneapolis.

James walked into Augies finding Dino at the bar. They peopled watch and chopped it up about nothing in general. In the middle of their conversation, a tall skinny chick approached them trying to make light conversation mixed with some flirting. But they both knew she was looking for a free drink. She focused on James and they talked for a bit and based on the conversation they had, James figured he could use her for what he had planned. He asks her what she was drinking. Turning to the bar, he ordered two long island ice teas. Dino took that as an opportunity to head towards the stage. Taking a seat where Dino was just sitting, she introduces herself as Shaniqua. A mother of now three, her youngest was just an infant. James smiled because he loved kids. They talked some more about life. She shared that she was just released from Shakopee prison on an assault charge for tasing her ex—boyfriend. James was amused, she was rough around the edges and he liked that. James asks if she wanted to go grab something to eat. Just like any other female, she accepted the food offer. Walking away from the bar, James found Dino and told him he was out. James and Shaniqua left and went to Denny's in Brooklyn Park.

***

Things started to move real fast. Money was flowing and James needed to keep a low profile. Toni got a call from her daughter, while at dinner. Her boyfriend got pulled over in the car she rented for him and it was towed. James was livid. He had previously told Toni to stop renting cars for dude. They got into a heated argument—having to leave the restaurant early, grabbing her grandchildren they left. Driving to Toni house, James phone started to blow up. Not answering it, pist Toni off. She must have forgot whom she was dealing with, because she swung on James. *"What the fuck?"* he screamed—snatching her coat and pulling it over her head, he pinned her down between the gearshift and console. "Man, you done lost your damn mind," Driving the rest of the way in this position, Toni tried to get out of James grip. Wiggling her head, she managed to hit it a couple times leaving bruise marks on her forehead. Once they made it to her house, she cried wolf and told her kids James hit her. Thinking she would call the police, he grabbed the work he had hid there and left. At this moment the relationship was over.

Knowing he should have gone home, after stopping at a stash house to drop what he had on him. Looking to clear his mind he, hit up Shaniqua. Knowing he would need stash houses. It was time to fully get on is shit. Over the next couple of months the two got to know each other more. When dealing with a street nigga. You're never asked to be his girl. You just ride shotgun while he bend a couple corners. Then he asks if you're hungry and now you're his boo. At this point, Shaniqua had moved into James house with her three children. While things were move super fast for James in the drug game, Shaniqua insecurities were taking over her. Ignoring the fact that James kept an extremely cleaned house. This all lead to late night arguments and his two younger children coming to him about how she was keeping the house nasty.

Slowly growing apart, James express that he needed another place to stash his work and that he was going to put her in her own place. She wasn't happy but felt that the relation ship wasn't over. So she agreed to the move. But the drama didn't end. The arguments gotten worst—he was tired of her stressing him about changing his lifestyle and the mental emotional abuse. While coming home late one night, he walked in his room to find Shaniqua lying in his bed. Not trying to fight he lay down and attempt to go to sleep. As soon as his body began to relax and was nearly in a deep sleep. She sat up questioning him where he was and why he was coming in so late. One of James packages came back short and he was aggravated. He completely ignore her, this pist her off even more to where she slapped him on the back of his head. James had enough. This was the last woman who thought she could lay hands him. He jumped up with his first mind to beat the shit out of her. But realized that this could send him to jail and violate his probation. Looking Shaniqua in the eyes with so much anger, he spoke calm words that would crush her soul, "You are not the type of woman I can consider marrying. I am going to find a woman and make her my wife. I need you to give me my house key back and leave."

Tears filled her eyes and the cold stare James gave told the truth that the relationship was over. Shaniqua grabbed her purse, threw the key on the bed and walked out of James house for the last time. Following behind her, he locked his door.

~Making Changes~

Waking up Sunday morning; Kianne boys were at her mom's house. She decided to head to church. It had been a couple of Sundays, so it was much needed. The devil had been living on her shoulders. Nothing in life seemed to be going right. Just purchasing a truck when the transmission went out a week later. It was sitting in the shop until she was able to get the money to get it out. She asked Orlando, one of her sponsors to send a couple of dollars to take care of it. Thankfully, he told her he would head to Western Union later that day.

Kianne was with her boys' father her entire teen life, she

was at a point where a relationship wasn't what she wanted. For seven years all she knew was Jairo. Being head over heels, doing things she thought she would never do. Love made you do some crazy shit. Jairo was four years older than her and, of course, linked to the south side Bloods. Although he had a legitimate job, he was also in the streets. Ever since Kianne could remember, she got whatever she wanted and was taken care of. If it wasn't her older sister Keila, it was her brother Levon and one of his women. Then came Jario. But after having to handle his work at times, then the ass whooping's, and disrespect, Kianne said fuck a relationship. For six years, Kianne lived a no relationship life. Working hard and party even harder. Well, that was until Kianne started talking to Rameir. He made her want more out of life. Taking her back to the beginning when there was love and goals set between Jario and herself. Wanting to change her ways, Kianne looked into more important things such as her credit. Already in college she cut the clubbing some. After two years Kianne thought Rameir would've wanted more than what they had. She enjoyed what they shared but was tired of sneaking him in her own house. They played the "we're together but not— we're not in a relationship, but you can't talk to no one else. But I'm going to continue dealing with my child's mother on the low." If only Cali would've stop playing with her emotions. Kianne met Cali when she was 19, fresh out of a sheltered relationship. She met him through Flex, one of her brother childhood home boys. With Cali, they had an understanding, no strings attached. But she was now ready to settle down. Six years later Cali gave her the same ole crap. Kianna put her thoughts aside, rolled out of bed to get ready for church. Kianne laid her clothes on the bed and got in the shower. Nice and fresh, she pranced around the house naked, letting herself air dry. Spraying on some Gucci Envy and slipped into a black lace Victoria's Secret panties and matching bra. After getting dressed, Kianne went downstairs, called a cab and waited. Ten minutes later her cab arrived, and they drove the eight minute ride to church in silence.

The driver pulled up in front of the church's white brick building, Kianne could hear Mother teaching Sunday school walking through the doors. She sat behind Sister Tina and her beautiful girls in the third pew from the altar. Listening to Mother teach, her mind began to wander about life and what changes needed to be made. Everything was going wrong and just because she prayed every night and attended church didn't make it okay. Sunday school was over before she pulled her thoughts together. Minister Brown came out to open services. Clearing her mind to focus on service—Kianne chimed in low singing the Morning Prayer and listened to the morning testimonies while clapping and singing with the praise team. After the choir sang, they took up the offering. The pastor began his sermon. "Single, Saved and Satisfied!" was his topic. "Was he listening in to my thoughts?" Kianne thought. The Pastor was preaching, and she knew the message was for her. He touched every issue Kianne was having. Before Pastor dismissed service. He made an announcement regarding his birthday service Friday night. Leaving church, Kianne heart was set on change. She now had a new look on lifewanting to make some changes. She felt the need to let people go—wanted to focus on becoming saved. No need for explanations—merely cutting people off was best for her. That included telling Orlando not to send me any more money. Ready to turn over a new leaf, get focused and work on myself as a woman, a mother and maybe a wife. She knew things had to change for the better and it started with her.

~Love at First Sight~

The week flew by quickly and it was Pastor's birthday, April 30th, 2010. Kianne had planned to attend the birthday service after work. When she left work, she took a cab home and called her mom to see if they could pick her up. She wanted to use the truck to attend service. It was irritating because it was never a friendly gesture. While on the phone with her mom— Tia, her home girl sent a texted. Tia boo from Chicago was in town, and they were heading to Seven Ultra Lounge. Well, there goes Friday night service Kianne thought. She was a work in progress. Her step dad picked her up and she drove back to her mom's house. Leaving the boys with her step dad—she headed to Macy's to find something to wear for that night. When she pulled up to Maplewood Mall, Rameir called. Of course he would call when I am about to head out. It never fails. He was always on me about stepping out. Ignoring the fact that I slowed down for him. But our situation wasn't moving in the direction I wanted too. I never thought then, but it may have been a sign. I ignored his call and continued shopping. Finding some Apple Bottom jeans and a yellow Apple Bottom shirt. Paying for my things I drove back to my mom's to get the boys, then headed home.

Rameir called again, and she ignored it. Tia called to tell her she was on her way. That girl had no sense of direction—she made it around 9:30 pm, after taking her an hour to get Kianne house. "Girl, as many times you been to my house, you still getting lost!"

"I know," she giggled. "It's dark out so I can't see where I'm going. But you're driving back!"

"Ok, cool."

Kianne told her niece who lived with her and who was babysitting, that she was heading out. Driving to Seven Ultra Lounge, Kianne got a text from Rameir asking what she was up too. "What's up," Kianne replied becoming a little irritated. A debate was coming once he found out where she was heading. But knowing she had to work in the morning, Kianne needed to ask him for a ride. And asking him was like asking for a million bucks. Ignoring his texted she replied asking Rameir for a ride. He replied that he was in Rosemount. Getting more irritated with her situation, she sped up to get to the lounge. He asked where she was again. With a smile Kianne replied, "Heading out." He didn't reply, and she knew he wouldn't. *Good!* She thought. Food and conversation would help clear her head.

Kianne drove up to valet. Walking into Seven, they headed straight to the bathroom. Fixing their hair and makeup, they took a couple of pictures, then headed to the second floor. The place was super packed. They walked to the bar—Kianne ordered two glasses of Pinot. Walking through the crowd, Tia spotted her baby daddy with his new girl. "Girl, do you see this nigga?"

"Not tonight! Don't be on no bullshit."

"I'm a just go say hi,"

"No!" I wasn't with the bullshit and talked Tia out of whatever she had in her head. They found a spot in front of a

VIP booth, stopped there and people-watched. Rameir was steady texting her with questions—asking she was at. She ignored him and gestured to Tia to head to the roof. As they were heading towards the stairs, some dude grabbed my arm. Pulling back and looking at this guy like he was shit on my shoe—I headed up the stairs.

The cool breeze hit me. I walked to the edge of the building and did a little more people-watching. Someone bumped me again—looking back I didn't see anyone. Nudging Tia, we walked to the other side of the roof top. The song "There Goes My Baby" by Usher came on; Kianne stopped and started to dance. Tia posted herself on the back of the VIP couch. As I was winding my hips, there was a soft touch on her shoulder, followed by a soft voice. "Hi beautiful, would you and your girls like to have this VIP table? We're about to leave." Before Kianne could decline, a drunk friend of Tia just happens to join our conversation, handing me her phone and telling me to take a picture. She grabbed the guy by his arm and told him to pose. I laughed to myself. He looked constipated. I took a couple of shots and was about to leave until he stopped me. Asking if I knew the girl.

"She's a friend of a friend."

He laughed as the girl danced offbeat to the music. Leaning against the wall, the guy took a step toward her; she could tell he was taking her all in. His eyes stayed on hers. As he got closer, his luscious lips parted as he prepared to speak. "Beautiful, smile, no need for the evil expressions."

"I'm annoyed."

"What's your name?"

"Kianne," stating dryly. She wasn't interested, and was already experiencing issues in the none relationship she was in.

"Hello Kianne, I'm James, James Earl."

With a stank face, she responded. "Hello."

"Beautiful, you sound so despondent? You stepped out tonight, so enjoy yourself."

"I'll try." I began to turn and walk away when he reached for my hand and stuck a piece of paper in it. I smiled and politely gave it back to him. "I'm sorry, but I can sincerely tell you I won't call."

"Well, can I have your number, and I'll call you?" I started to give him a phony number, but something told me to do otherwise. I must admit he was sexy. But there was something more drawing him to me. He shook my hand and said he would call me. As James and the people he was with walked off, I sat my crying feet down—helped myself to the bottle he left and enjoyed the rest of the night.

~Who Are You~

Getting up for work was rough. Although she didn't start till 10 am. Kianne was extremely tired, and had no business going out the night before. Barely making it on time. The day was busy the moment she arrived. One girl called off, and with four stylists'— they were juggling multiple clients. Between several perms and a few colors— Kianne tips were great, but her feet were barking. The stylist's managed to take in almost every walk in that day and thirty minutes pass closing, they were able to go home and Kianne was grateful. Having Sunday and Monday off, she planned to enjoy every bit of it. Making it home, she checked in on her boys who were in bed. She took a long, hot bath, crawled into bed and drifted off.

***

Sunday morning, the boys and Kianne made it to church on time. The pastor was still preaching on "Single, Saved and Satisfied." Kianne was taking notes and planning her life to move forward. After service, she cooked the only meal the boys honestly ate: macaroni and cheese with fried chicken and biscuits. They watched a movie while they ate dinner, then Kianne laid down to relax. As she laid in bed, her phone rang— looking at the number, she wondered who in the hell was calling. She answered on the fourth ring. To her surprise it was James. Kianne forgot all about him. His sexy voice made her smile from within. After going back and forth with Rameir the past couple of months, his soft tone was relaxing.

"How was your day, beautiful?"

"It was just another day— made it to church and now I'm relaxing. I have a lot on my mind. I'm ready to head to bed."

"That's not good. Since today is practically over, how can I make it a better day tomorrow?"

"Well, tomorrow I'm off, and I love food, so we can do lunch." Kianne thoughts begin to have a battle with her spirit. Here I go again. But he pursued me, so I'm not chasing.

"Cool, cool, I got some business to take care of in Saint Paul and have no clue about where I'm going. How about you show me around and I'll take you to lunch?"

"That sounds good."

James had so much going on— Kianne could hear kids and a lot of talking going on in the background. They talked for a bit longer, until she got irritated with the side conversations. Kianne gave him her address and told him she was going to sleep and to call in the morning when he was on the way. She told him her kids left for school at 8 am, and he could come around that time.

James showed up the next morning around 8:30. The boys had left, but since he was here, Kianne asked him to ride toward the school. Driving up Arkwright Street, toward Bruce Ventos Elementary School. She saw the boys, and they pulled up beside them. Dropping them off at school, they headed to the Downtowner to wash his car.

Kianne turned to James and asked him what made him ask for her number after she was so rude to him. "I could tell that you were irritated, and you didn't want to be there. Which made me feel like that was not your scene. A woman that doesn't want to be in a club setting is a good thing for a man."

"Oh, I guess." Chuckling, if he only knew. "What is it that you do for a living?"

"I started a snow plowing and landscaping business a year or so ago. What about yourself?"

"I am a full—time student studying Criminal Justice. Not sure at the moment where I want to go in the field. And I'm a hair stylist at Serenity Beauty Salon." Kianne asked him how many kids he had, where he was from, where he grew up and what made him move to Minnesota. He answered mentioning he had four kids and a grandbaby, born in California, lived in Monroe, LA till he was about twelve and later moved to Minnesota.

They pulled up in the car wash line and the attended approached them. James chose a service and, they got out of the truck to go pay. He had asked Kianne if she wanted anything. Walking on his left side, she read the name on his hat: "JAMES EARL." slowly repeating the name out loud. Kianne eyes got big as she thought, this couldn't be. Unsure how she missed it at the club when he told her his name. James had a slight smile on his face as he asked why she said his name like that. Again she thought this could not be the

"James Earl" that they said shot One—leg Edward—the same "James Earl" that I just did my research paper on. I laughed out loud and called his name. "*JAMES EARL*—you got to be fucking kidding me." I stepped closer to him and whispered,

"You shot Edward!"

His lips were curved upward, mouth partly open, showing his perfect white teeth. With a smile that said, Yes! I'm James Earl. "Yes, baby girl, I'm James Earl— but I did not shoot Edward. In fact, the shorter version of that story is... Cutting him off, Kianne blurted out, "there was an eyewitness who testified that the shooter was six feet or six feet five inches, dark—skinned, with a shotgun. The forensics proves your innocence. Edward just lied on the stand. I did my research on the case."

"I see."

They pulled James truck up and they headed to Kianne's favorite restaurant. She was still in shock but anxious to experience more of James Earl.

Sitting at the table with four other visitors at Benihana's, James looked deep into Kianne eyes, expressing what he was searching for out of life. He was looking for a woman to love him for him and Kianne was praying for a companion to cherish her past her physical elements. With James, Kianne was able to be herself, no hidden agenda, no lies needed to be told. They talked about her childhood, teen parenting, domestic relationship, dating married men and athletes. Kianne opened up her soul, showed him her wounds. He knew Kianne's life story by the time they finished with their food. His conversation was exciting; he spoke from his soul. They had so much in common. The picture he painted— Kianne saw herself in it. High off his every word, Kianne blurted out, "You're going to be my husband"

She caught him off guard. He laughed and asked if she been smoking. "If I'm high, it's off either the bullshit you're telling me or the dreams you're selling." He laughed again, but she was dead ass. He was going to be her husband. She looked James in the eyes and told him they were getting married. Surely he thought I lost my mind at that point. But I felt it in my heart.

After eating her plate and some of James', he took care of the bill. They drove back to Kianne's house. James asked why she wasn't driving. "I sliced one too many car tires in my past life and karma caught up to me." She mumbled. He gave her a strange look. "My car is in the shop, and I need $1800 to get it out. I'm a thousand dollars short." James told Kianne to call the people and tell them She was on the way to pick up her truck. He pulled out a knot of hundreds and counted out twenty. "Here beautiful, you can pay me back here and there. But you need your truck." Kianne was thankful and agreed to pay him back. But knowing he was going to be her husband, shewasn't worried about it.

A week went by; they spoke on the phone almost every night since their first date. They went to dinner and movies nearly every other night, and James had popped up to her job a few times to take her to get ice cream on break. Teenage love and it was sweet. He later expressed that he wanted to take this further. He explained that he had broken up with his crazy ex—girl months ago. The things she did made him a little cautious about moving quickly into another relationship, but Kianne presence made him feel safe. He was relaxed around her. Their relationship grew deep and strong overnight. It felt as if they were together for years. When her coworkers asked how long they been dating, she had to think back and count the days from when they first met. In just a matter of four weeks James and Kianne were as one. She stopped seeking and began to pray for what she wanted, the Lord blessed her with him. Despite his past, she needed him, and he needed her. The long phone conversations, bringing flowers and lunch to work was more than she had ever received within a healthy relationship. Kianne loved every gesture he made.

***

On Memorial Day in the wee hours. James called and said he was on the way to her house. She went to unlock the door and climbed back in bed. Later woken by James kissing her on the forehead. She rolled over to James on one knee. I slightly sitting up, looking at James through sleepy eyes. "Bae, I have never felt this way about a woman in my life. When I am with you, I am at peace. In my heart, you are the one I want to spend the rest of my life with. Although it has only been a month, it feels as if we have been together a life time. I don't want to go on with you just being my woman. Kianne Johnson, will you be my wife?"

James pulled out a ring and placed it on my finger. I was completely speechless. I jumped up out of the bed and kissed him gently and whispered, "Yes!" We kissed and hugged— tears of joy fell down my face. I had expressed before that marriage was against my religion. But James was able to change that. James and I crawled into my bed and cuddled until we fell asleep in each other's arms.

The sunshine crept through the curtains. Waking up with a smile on her face. Leaping out of bed, Kianne got in the shower and got myself ready for the day. They were hosting Memorial Day at Como Park. The boys and James slept as Kianne prepared the food they were bringing. She cleaned and seasoned the chicken, spaghetti was cooked, and baked beans were ready to go. As Kianne packed the cooler, James came strolling down the stairs, kissed her on the neck and said he would meet them there to announce their engagement. Little did he know she had already taken a picture and placed it on Facebook with a caption. "New beginnings—a token of his love!" You know when you post on Facebook, the negativity follows. Inbox messages and text messages came with questions and opinions, and I ignored them all.

Unsure of how the family would take it. To hear them tell it, I was a young Jezebel. Sharing my new relationship was a big step beside my kids' father and Cortez, who my kids' aunt and first lady wanted me to marry. I never brought another man around. I kept my personal life to myself.

***

Levon was on the grill, the kids were playing at the park and Kianne sisters, herself along with their mom was talking.

James rolled up in his sparkling blue 1967 Cutlass plus one. Kianne pull Levon aside, so he could check the dude out. She never trust anyone and wasn't feeling him bringing extras around.

Kianne introduced James to everyone, then turned around and announced that we were getting married, holding her beautiful piece of bling in the air. Everyone seemed cool with it. Now all there was left to do was tell his kids.

Unsure how that would go since she just popped up out of nowhere. James' daughter was 16 years old. Kianne was 25 and still a daddy's girl at heart. She understood where her feelings about her daddy's new relationship would come from. After the BBQ the boys left with her mom and later that night Kianne drove over to his apartment off East River Road and Highway 694. Not knowing he had kids over. Walking into his apartment she saw a light-skinned teenage version of James sitting at the dining room table. Kianne laughed to myself. "Hey Jamie, how's your mom and sister?"

Who would have thought my little cousin would be his son? I know it sounds crazy, just as crazy as his daughter being my older two boys' cousin. But let's just go with common law marriage. My uncle was with Jamie's aunt for a decade and three kids later. We're not blood cousins, but we are family. Jamie looked at me strangely, like who the hell is she talking to and questioning me about my people. James laughed; I explained I was Pumpkin and them cousin from their dad's side. It was awkward but one down and three more to go.

.

~Warning Signs~

It had been a few weeks since James proposed to Kianne. Setting a wedding date for May 2011, Kianne begin to plan their big day. Scheduling a few appointments to look at the many mansions Minnesota offered as venues'. Kianne was now sitting at home watching TV when she got a call from James asking to go pick up his daughter from the house. The panic in his voice scared her. Unsure of what was going on— the sound of his tone told her it wasn't good. Kianne rushed to his house and picked up his daughter. While driving from the north side, Kianne brother asked her to stop by. She drove his way for a quick talk. As she pulled up to her brother's apartment on Larpenter and Rice Street, she called to tell him she was outside. Levon came out the building and stood at the curb as Kianne parked her truck. "What's up bro?"

"Man, nothing good. I spoke with our cousin Jase." Levon told Kianna things she knew nothing about. Things she should have never discovered from her brother. What he mentioned was disturbing, and Kianna realized at that moment things were about to turn for the worse. Three hours had passed before James called. He told Kianne to drop his daughter off and meet him at Applebee's. She rushed through traffic—leaving the boys with his daughter, then headed to Fridley. When she finally reached him, they grabbed a table and ordered food. Well, Kianne ordered food. Looking her in the eyes James told her the Feds had been following him all day through the Northside. He thought for sure he was going to get picked up today and didn't want his baby girl at the house. "Thank you for going to get her."

"No problem. So—tell me what's up?" James laid everything out. Explaining that his past was catching up to him. This was news she didn't want to hear. Kianne wasn't stupid. Living a life that allowed her to spend five thousand a day, knowing lawn care wasn't footing the bill. Kianne told James what her brother said. And explained the background of their cousin. Giving James a forewarning that whatever was going on, while the other receives the calm before the storm, he would see the aftermath. It never crossed James mind that all this would transpire. It never does. Now it was only a matter of time. He needed to cover his ass.

With all the information Kianne was giving, she had to determine whether to remain with James or move on with her life. After eating her food, she drove to James house and he went about his business.

By the time James made it home that night. Kianne had made up in her mind that she would love him regardless and move forward with the wedding. With that said, they moved the wedding date to September 18, 2010, leaving eight weeks to plan it. Kianne reminded James that she had yet to meet his mother. When she mentioned this, he made arrangements for them to visit Monroe, LA with Black. Why did he have to go and why was he always around? Kianne didn't like him and his sneaky ways bother her. James told her about the police car that was following Black the other night and that he found a tracking device on Black's car. How could he not notice an unknown object on his car? James felt that it was best to keep tabs on Black, so he wanted him to tag along. Yet days before they were to leave—Black was nowhere to be found. James had been calling him and was getting upset that he couldn't get ahold of the nigga. Jase called James, he heard Black got picked up on a parole violation and that the Feds had him in questioning. The day we were leaving, Black called to tell him he went camping with his girl and he couldn't get any reception where he was. Kianne called bullshit, but it was not her place to say. James was walking around the house nose flared, eyes squinted and dark, like a storm was brewing inside him. He needed to see what was up with his man. In the room packing, Kianne pulled James to the bed and straddled him. "Listen, don't let all this upset you and ruin our getaway. We're going to visit with your parents, keep an eye on Black and get back to planning our wedding."

"Babe, I'm trying, but things don't seem right with dude."

"I understand but don't stress; besides it makes you look old. I need you to look as young as possible for my pictures."

"Your pictures, HUH?"

Kianne tilted my head to the side. Slightly rising then rotating her hips, she smiled. "Woman, don't do that unless you plan on giving it up."

Laughing, Kianne climbed off James and finished packing their bags. Then double-checked to make sure she had everything and went to get in the car. James nephew was in the driver's seat waiting to drop them off. They drove 25 minutes through light traffic, arriving at the airport and went through the security checkpoint. As they boarded the plane, James noticed Black was already seated. Settling on the plane, Kianne leaned her head on James' shoulder. Before the plane could leave the loading gate, she was fast asleep. James mind worried to the matter at hand. Black went missing, then shows up to catch his flight on time. Something wasn't right. for seventy 2 hours

They landed in Dallas for their connecting flight, merely having 8 minutes to get to Gate 17. "Why in the hell did I wear heels?" Kianne thought. James and Black ran through the airport as she speed-walked behind him. Barely making it, they boarded the small plane. In the matter of moments Kianne was sleep. But that hour and ten-minute ride was quick. She woke up sweaty as fuck. James grabbed their carry-on luggage and exited the plane. The airport was super small—right when they entered was the security, then the waiting area and the exit doors. Standing close to the exit doors was a short, heavyset woman and a tall, dark skinned man. I assumed that was his mom because she was waving our way. "Aww, look at this little thang. She's so tiny, James. Not as tiny as that other gal. But that's ok; you are in the right place. I'll have you nice in plump like me in no time. Just the way my baby likes his women. I'm so glad you got rid of that ole skinny-looking thang, looking like she was sick. Eyes were bulging out of her head, poor child." Kianne looked over at James with an angry face.

"Mom please, nobody wants to hear all that. My bae is beautiful the way she is. Kianne this is my mother Karen and my pops Joe."

"Hello!" Kianne spoke faintly. She was already irritated. Walking out the airport they all got into James's Suburban that was double parked and drove off. Pulling up to a shaggy old house with bags of water hanging from the roof. Kianne tilted her head sideways—James whispers "it's keeping the flies away." With raised eyebrows, Kianne followed James as he walked into the house. The smell of mothballs filled their lungs. Thinking to herself, "Kianne hoped they weren't staying here." She pulled James's arm to ask what hotel they were staying at. He smiled and said, "Here" Squinting her eyes, and biting her bottom lip—this was going to be a long weekend.

After getting settled in, James took Kianne around the town along with Black. He introduced her to his sister Monique, her husband and their children. They drove through the neighborhoods he grew up in, his old schools and places he hung out at as a child. Monroe, LA, was a tiny town. It felt like a Freddie nightmare, driving in circles, going one direction, only to end up back at the same place you started.

Back at his mother's house James was bragging about Kianne's cooking. She wasn't no chef, but she can move around in the kitchen. His mom must have felt same type of way.

"Oh, I know how to cook chicken without flour. Ain't that what you said—she don't use flour? Y'all want me to cook some chicken?" Black sat with a grin enjoying every minute of Karen's silent competition. He knew James mother well. Kianne sat next to James thinking, realizing that there was going to be a battle between the two. Karen loved her baby boy and any women was a threat to their relationship. Kianne whispered to James "I'm not eating here."

James started to talk his way to the door, his mom asked were we staying for dinner. As soon as James advised no, she went to tearing up. Kianne rolled my eyes. Was she serious?

"Mama Kay, I'm a stay here with y'all while the two love birds step out for some alone time." Black spoke.

James and Kianne pulled up to Red Lobster to eat. There weren't many restaurants to choose from besides Olive Garden and Applebee's. There was no wait when we walked in—the waitress greeted and showed us our seats. As soon as we sat down James's phone rang. Kianne immediately ordered a glass of wine and began to look the menu over. She wasn't trying to ear hustle, but of course, my ears were open. He had a look on his face, that look of someone asking for something. "Ok, I'll call you back," Kianne kicked him because she heard a female voice reply, "Thank you."

"That was Ray's mom. She needed a couple of dollars to get to Memphis."

"I'm sure it's regarding her sister."

"Yeah, they need to get down there to bury her."

James called his son to take his mom some money to leave town. They chatted a little longer, then got off the phone. Soon the waitress came and took their order. The food arrived, and they ate in silence. Kianne could tell he had a lot on his mind. Whatever it was, she prayed it wasn't beyond his control. They finished eating and headed back to his mom's.

When they pulled up into his mom's driveway, her and Joe were sitting on the porch smoking cigarettes. James walked up to his mom and hugged her, Kianne said hey and bypassed them to walk in the house. She was full and wanted to lie down. As she stripped and went to lie in the bed, Kianne saw something crawling. As she pulled the covers, whatever it was started to fly. A high pitch scream escapes her mouth—it was a flying roach. James came in with a grin, looking at Kianne's naked flesh. "Yeah, Bae, I can't stay here. I saw a flying roach, and it went over there somewhere. I'm going to a hotel."

James laughed. "Bae, it's just a bug."

"Well, you sleep with it!" Kianne shook her bag out and put her clothes back in it, grabbed the keys and headed to the car. James followed behind. As they walked through the living room, James told Black they were heading to get a room. His mom walk in the front door with Joe on her tail. "Hey, where are you guys going now?" his mother whined.

"Kianne wants to get a hotel for the night—we'll be back in the morning since our flight leaves late." His mom went to tear up as if she would never see him again. Kianne rolled her eyes and went to the car. Several minutes later James came out the back door as his mom stood at the front door staring, watching as they drive off. They headed to the Hilton in West Monroe. Kianna laid on the bed and turned on "Forensic Files." James crawled up behind, and before the show was over, he was asleep. Kianne grabbed his phone and went through his call log. There was nothing out of the ordinary. She put his phone back and went to sleep.

Kianne woke up around 9 am. James was on the phone talking. Pulling the covers back, Kianne showed her naked flesh. He smiled and told whoever he was talking to he would call them back. James placed his phone on the table, then slid back in bed for breakfast.

James jumped up to the sound of the hotel phone. Looking at the clock, it was noon. He answered the phone and requested a 3 pm late checkout. They got in the shower and got dressed. James called his mom to tell her they were on the way and to be ready to go eat.

They picked up Black and his parents and found a mom and pop restaurant down the street—called Big Momma's Fine Foods. Kianne ordered smothered pork chops and James frowned. They sat down to eat. Discussing the wedding with his parents. His mother gave Kianne a hard time. She didn't want to fly, the drive was too long, and she wanted to wear white. This rubbed Kianne the wrong way. Ready to get back to Minnesota. Not taking James as a mama's boy—she had no idea there were going to be issues between her and his mother.

~Wedding-Planning~

Once they made it back to Minnesota; Kianna was in wedding plan mode. Her wedding dress and the bridesmaids dress had been ordered. The invites were being overnighted and the venue was booked. Kianne was still waiting for James guest list and for him to get his groomsmen together. While she laid across her bed jotting notes, she heard the front door open. A smile crept across her face. She turned over on her back listening to the footsteps of her future husband. The bedroom door swung opened and Kianne eyes extended out her head. "What the hell are you doing here Cali?"

"Well, it's nice to see you too, hot pocket."

"Nah, you got to go. You can't stay here or be here. You

have to go before my fiancé gets back"

"Well damn. You really getting married."

"I am, and you have to leave *right* now."

"Okay! Okay. I just came to give you this and return your key."

"You couldn't call to meet up? Whatever— it doesn't matter. Now leave." Cali handed me a gift bag and my spare key. "Wait, I can't take this."

"You haven't even looked inside it."

"It doesn't matter, it's a gift and I don't want to have to explain this shit."

"Well, I'm not leaving until you accept it!"

"Fine, thank you. I'll open it later and call you, now leave!"

"If I don't hear from you soon— I'm coming to your job." Kianne rushed Cali out the house. As he was walking to his car James was walking up. They looked each other down. Seeing that Cali had a smirk on his face. James began to jog to the door. He pushed Kianne aside and headed upstairs to the bedroom. She closed the door, shaking her head. Before she could turn around, James was back downstairs in her face with a gift bag and a stack of hundreds. Eyes squinted, nose flared, James spat out, "What the fuck is this?" Kianne walked past him and went upstairs into the bedroom, trying to buy some time to avoid the issue at hand. He was right on my tail. *"You didn't hear me the first time? What the fuck is this shit?"*

"You don't have to yell. Looks like a purse and some money. I had no idea that was in the gift bag— I didn't know he was coming over. The nigga just showed up. He wouldn't leave unless I accepted the gift. So, I did."

"I have been outside for twenty minutes. I saw when the nigga pulled up and walked into your house like he lived here. The only light that was on was the bedroom. You still fucking the nigga?

"No! You see the wedding planner and a plate of fruit on the bed. I thought it was you coming in. I fucking forgot he had a key!"

James walked in the bedroom as she followed. He turned towards her. "You won't be needing this shit! Call the nigga and give it back!"

Kianne sighed, knowing this wasn't over. She headed

downstairs to the kitchen to fix him a plate of the cabbage, rice, chicken, and cornbread she cooked earlier. Placing his food in the microwave, her phone rang. "I'm going back to Cali," played out— then the doorbell rang. Kianne didn't move.

James came down the stairs with her phone in hand. Peeking around into the kitchen, he gave an evil look and then walked into the living room and answered the door. It was the boys being dropped off by their dad. Kianne went back to her room and climbed in the bed. James followed with his plate and ate in silence— it was killing Kianne.

James sat next to her and explained that he trusted and believed in her. He kissed her on the forehead and said goodnight. Grabbing the spare key off the dresser, he closed the door. Heading out the front door, he told the boys he loved them and good night.

Kianne prayed this wouldn't be a restless night. The drama Cali caused and planning the wedding, her mind was all over the place. She rolled over and closed her eyes. But all she could think about was the wedding being five weeks away. When her mind finally rested, tt felt as if she just drifted off to sleep. Kianne woke up to James staring her in the face at five am.

"You know, when I want to be mad, I can't even do that. Knowing that you love me for me makes me smile within."

"I'm glad you came back." Not wanting to deal with the issues from earlier. She turned the focus on their wedding.

"I need your guest list and groomsmen list." Kianne rolled over to check her text messages. She had texted her bridesmaids yesterday about their hair appointments. One was difficult. She wanted her mother to do her hair, which was understandable. Kianne wanted her stylist to do everyone's hair. Tia texted back saying that her mom would still do her hair. She asked James if he wanted to get married in Vegas. To her surprise, he said yes. Kianne was over the back—and—forth with everyone. One of her friends of many years backed out. This said all she needed to know about where their friendship stood. They set the date for September 18, 2010. Kianne grabbed her laptop from the nightstand and booked flights. James called his mom and got the information needed. Kianne called her dad to explain what was going on and to get is information to book his flight. She then sent a mass text to let everybody know they canceled the wedding. After searching chapels in Vegas. Kianne found the perfect location—including James' request to have it outside. She booked a limo and made other arrangements for their trip. Kianne made sure they were staying longer than their parents. She knew his mother would work her last nerve.

~Attempting Vegas~

Kianne could sense something was nagging James. It was three in the morning and he was pacing the floor in the family room, checking his phone every couple of minutes. Kianne watched him from his bedroom, while packing their things for the wedding. Since the first run in with the Feds, she's been staying at his place. They were leaving in a few hours and for once everything was going as planned.

"Bae, can you settle down, please?"

"Some things aren't adding up. Why is it harder when you're trying to keep your nose clean?"

"I don't know but you need to calm down. Your bags

are packed and so you are good to go. I have to pick up my mom. Our flight leaves at 7 am. Please don't miss your flight; yours leaves at 10 am! This means you need to be there at 8:30 am and no later." I had a feeling he would be late, but I was giving him the benefit of the doubt. I kissed him on the cheek and left to pick up my mom.

Kianne left her mom's place with the kids in tow, heading to the park-n-go parking lot. From there they took the shuttle to the airport. At the Delta lane kiosk, attempting to print their tickets. The screen read there was no reservation. Kianne went to the desk, and the clerk said the tickets were canceled. "Are you serious?" The lady said the travel agency canceled. I was beyond irate. Booking three flights, which cost fifth-teen hundred dollars. Kianne was pist since it was part of the spending money she took out of savings. After purchasing the tickets, they made it through security with no issues. Boarding started at 8:50 am, when the time came, they were told the flight was booked, and they were put on standby. Kianne started to have a nervous breakdown.

James came trolling through the crowd. She hadn't spoken to him since early that morning. He spotted the boys and came their way. Walking up to Kianne he asks, "Aren't y'all supposed to be in Vegas?"

"They canceled the boys' and my mom's flights and I had to purchase them again. For some reason, my debit card was not charged."

Once James sat down the flight attendant called Kianne's name. Rushing to the podium to see what she wanted. Of course, she wanted to advise she had seats for all of them. Didn't think of it at the time. But it was all a setup, and the flights were never canceled. How was it that there were no seats available until James made it to the airport? They boarded their flight and got settled on the plane. Her mom sat in the front of the plane while the boys, James and Kianne sat toward the back.

***

They made it to Vegas around 2 pm. Kianne's daddy and James' parents arrived just as we were leaving the airport. James damned near flipped out when he found out that Kianne didn't rent a vehicle. Taking the shuttle to the hotel. He ended up going back to the airport to get one, his parents stayed and waited on him. My dad took a cab and met them at Circus Circus hotel. Kianne checked into the three rooms that were reserved for the parents and the kids. Once they were settled, she took a cab to the Venetian to check into Her and James room.

Now that everyone was settled in, James and Kianne drove to get their parents and kids then went to IHOP to eat. Sitting around the table, there were about three different conversations going on. Kianne happened to catch the one her dad and James were having just as he gave her dad his cell phone to look at cars. Before Kianne could scream the words out, *"Don't scroll,"* it was too late. Her daddy dropped James' phone on the table.

"Geesh, that wasn't no car. I have seen my little girl naked, but I didn't want to see her like that," he blurted out. As black as she was, Kianne face was red. Already knowing what photo he saw—face down, ass up. It was the worst feeling ever. Thankful the food came so they could eat and kill that awkward moment. While eating, they discussed the weekend that was ahead of them.

~Wedding Day~

Just like black families—James and Kianne, were running late. They had some last minute items to pick up for their wedding day. James's mom also mentioned that she had nothing to wear. Kianna was sure it was the fact that she wanted something new. After she had been told what they were wearing. She had the nerve to say she wanted a white dress to wear. The woman had lost her mind. What made her think she would be in white on my wedding day? They all went to the Fashion Show Mall. While the guys wandered off somewhere in the mall. Kianne took her soon to be mother in law, with her mom in tow to Macy's to find her something to wear. Everything that was showed to her, she didn't like. It was more the color. Kianne's mom was in gold, and she was given the option of silver or wisteria purple. Karen insisted on finding something white. Kianne rolled her eyes so much her head was hurting. "Listen you are not wearing white on my day. Karen you will have to wear what you have." Giving up, Kianne walked away. They were running late and had to go. She called James to meet them in the front so they could head to the hotel. The men went to our parent's room to get ready, while the ladies went to The Venetian. Kianne was nervous and excited and could barely control her emotions.

Once they got dressed, they headed to the chapel in the limo that was reserved. Kianne went straight into the bathroom to fix her hair and makeup. Moment's later; Kianne mom came and told her that they locked the boys in the room. Instead of going to the front desk— they panicked, which only meant they were over there drinking. Call my dad the ringleader, because I am sure that is who started it.

The men arrived twenty minutes passed the time they were suppose be there. As they rushed out of the cab— Kianne's mom went to let the director know that they were ready. Well, that was what they thought. James came to the bathroom door.

"Umm Babe, I am not sure what happened, but I can't find the marriage license. I think I left it in the cab."

"Are you kidding me, James?"

Not knowing if James was getting cold feet and he was trying to back out or if he really lost the licenses. Kianne wasn't angry, just irritated. Her dad came to the bathroom door to tell let them know they were trying to locate the cab driver. The clerk told James that the office didn't close until 12 am. When Kianne herd that, she dashed out of the bathroom, and ran to James telling him to come on. They would just have to pay the extra fee and get a new one. They got in the limo to head downtown. His mother, of course, wanted to tag along; Kianne's mom and dad stayed behind.

Making it downtown Vegas in about ten minutes. James and Kianne walked up the stairs into the office, with onlookers applauding; they got a duplicate license and headed back to the chapel. Feeling so many emotions at once, Kianne became nervous all over again. She was marrying the man she loved. The most important people were there, aside from her partying babies; who had passed out in the hotel.

When they made it back to the chapel, the minister was ready. The ceremony was a mimic of what was originally planned. It was outdoors with candlelight, white roses and Luther Vandross in the background. Kianne's dad walked her down the aisle, her new stepfather-in-law bore witness to the wonderful union by signing the marriage certificate. Halfway through the ceremony we looked toward the seats and saw that many strangers came to witness a magical night. James and Kianne looked at each other and smiled. Complete strangers supported them more than those who called themselves friends and family. Yet many that were sitting in the crowd weren't just strangers, but federal agents who have been following James since August.

After saying "I do" they headed to the limo. Kianne's dad started to grab a cab when Karen suggested they all ride in the limo. Kianne gave James the side-eye. He opened the door and got in, not realizing there was champagne on ice and chocolate-covered strawberries. He climbed in and slid to the back. Kianne followed as her mother and father and his parents crawled in after. James whispered, "Did you have something in mind?"

Kianne just stared with an attitude and ignored his question. Of course, as his mother got settled in her spot she leaned over, extremely happy to see food on the side panel. Taking deep breaths, this was not the way she wanted to start her morning as a married woman. It was 1:30 am in Vegas and the streets were crawling with excitement. Kianne had a room that was prepped, and things planned for the ride back to the hotel. But here she was in a limo with their parents, cruising Sin City on her wedding morning.

James instructed the driver to head to Circus Circus Hotel. As the driver was pulling up, James pulled several hundred-dollar bills out of his wallet and passed them around. Hoping it would keep them busy for the day. They all got out, as the driver drove James and Kianne back to their room. The ride was quiet; James rubbed Kianne's back as they rode down the strip. Pulling in front of the Venetian hotel, the driver walked around to open the door. As they were getting out of the limo, the driver gave Kianne a funny feeling. He stared as if he knew them. As he held the door, Kianne could have sworn she heard him say, "All right, JEEZY," which is one of the names James was supposed to go by according to federal documents. Staring into his eyes, Kianne asked, "I'm sorry, what did you say, sir?"

"HUH? I'm sorry. I said, "all right, you three," he replied as he looked to see if someone else was coming out. Kianne gave him the side-eye. There was something strange about him. James grabbed Kianne's left hand; lifting her dress with her right hand, they headed inside. People were congratulating them as they walked through the lobby. Getting on the elevator, James pulled his wife into him and they kissed, long and gentle. When the elevators stopped on their floor, Kianne pranced off backward, giving James a finger motion to follow. He came out of the elevator; it was all slow motion like he was MR. GQ. Turning around, Kianne ran to the room. He came up and grabbed her by the waist. She opened the door and he pushed her in. James locked the door behind him and followed Kianne to the bed.

Walking up behind her, he kissed the back of her neck. Slowly unzipping her dress, he whispered, "All I want to see you in is your wedding ring and diamond earrings."

Kianne smiled as she let the dress drop to the floor. James stepped back, seductively bending forward, Kianne slid her thong off and did the sexiest cat crawl on the bed.

***

The sun beamed in through the curtains, waking Kianne from her sleep. Rolling over to her side, running her tongue around her mouth while sniffing her top lip. Kianne smiled a smile of victory. Facing her new husband, she leaned in and kissed him. James wrapped his arm around her side. As she began to lean into him, his phone rang.

"Don't answer that."

"It's my mom; let me see what they want." Kianne rolled her eyes and straddled him.

"Good morning, Mom, what's up?" he answered.

"Oh, nothing—seeing what you two lovebirds are up to."

"Oh, we're still in bed about to order breakfast as soon as I get off the phone with you and hit the strip afterward."

"Were you guys coming down here?"

"No, Mom, today we're spending the day together. I'll call you when we get back to our room, and you all can come down before your flights leave."

"Ok honey, love you."

"Bye, Mom." James put his cell phone down and picked up the hotel phone to order breakfast. Kianne stood up to go to the bathroom. Leaning on the bathroom door, she asked, "*Was I not enough?*" James smiled.

After breakfast, James and Kianne got dressed and went out on the strip. They first took the gondola ride at their hotel. A couple just got off as the representative told them it would be a minute. They had to switch workers. It wasn't a thought at that time, but they later found out it was a federal agent guiding their canoe. Sitting back as the gondolier guided them through the maze; James and Kianne took pictures as they relaxed, enjoying the scenery. Right before they departed the ride, the gondolier took their picture as well. Ready to do some shopping, James retrieved the car from valet then drove to the Bellagio. It took forever to find parking. They could have just walked there.

The inside of the hotel was lovely; it had an indoor forest park, giving a very relaxing atmosphere. Strolling through the Bellagio hotel, Tiffany's was coming up. Kianne smiled within when James suggested that they go in. "Good afternoon," the sales rep said to them.

"Good afternoon! My wife would like to see the classic Tiffany set."

"Okay, let's look over here." The man walked to the counter and pulled out a "Return to Tiffany" heart tag necklace and placed it on me. I glanced into the mirror and smiled. Something that was so simple, yet beautiful.

"We will take it,"

"Babe, can I get the bracelet and earrings?" Kianne whined.

"No love, next time. Let's do some more shopping and we will come back." James paid for the necklace and they walked across to the Gucci store. James got a call as they entered the doors. Whatever the call was about bothered him. His eyes were squinted, and his nose flared, which meant the news wasn't good. Walking into the store, this black leather Gucci bag screamed Kianne's name. Asking the clerk to take it off the shelf. While looking at herself in the mirror, James came to her side.

"Yeah, I like that one. Sir, can you grab the matching wallet and ring these up, please?" Smiling within, Kianne followed James to the counter. He pulled his credit card out and handed it to the sales clerk to purchase the items. Kianne grabbed her new bag, and they walked out. Normally she would not have been able to walk out with a bag that easily. So, whoever called that had his mind elsewhere, Kianne thanked them silently.

After shopping, they called their parents to let them know we were on the way to pick them up. I wasn't ready to get back so soon. But they were leaving tomorrow morning and the least I could do was spend a little more time with his parents. We picked them up and went back to our room. James ordered a movie, and we all sat down to socialize. The boys were worn out. Staying up till morning. They laid on the floor and slept. His mom was doing more talking than watching. Kianne soul was anxious for her to leave. Snuggled in James' arms, she kissed her husband and told him she would be back.

Kianne made her way to the mall inside the hotel. Finding Victoria's Secret as soon as she exited the elevator. While Kianne was browsing, she couldn't help but notice a man strolling through the store. He seemed out of place. Here in Vegas at a Victoria's Secret store and he was in a suit? Pretty off key to her. She ignored it and kept it moving. Making her way to the Sephora store, heading to the perfume section. After she paid for her things, Kianne went to grab a drink in the casino area. Then went and sat at a slot machine and there again, the man in the suit. Feeling uneasy she went upstairs. Hoping the movie was over and they were ready to get back to their hotel to start packing. When she walked in the room, unfortunately that wasn't the case. James had ordered another movie before falling back into a coma. Their fathers were in deep conversation. Kianne slid in between her husband and his mom to finish the movie with them. She figured she would tell James about the man later.

Waking up in the bed confused, Kianne glanced at

the clock on the nightstand. It was 4 am and everyone was gone, including James. The poker tables must have called him in his sleep, or he never came back when he took everyone back to their rooms. I got up and got myself together and then went downstairs to look for James. As soon as I got off the elevator, I saw him at a poker table by some slots. I walked up behind him as he let out a sigh of frustration and irritation; he must have been losing.

"Love, you left me!"

"Yeah, my fault. After taking everyone to their rooms I thought I'd make back that money I spent today."

That was James' excuse to gamble and he was serious. But he was done; starting with $200 to play, he was up $2000 but walked away with $1100. It was better than nothing. Kianne grabbed a drink and they headed to the car to pick up their parents. Kianne dad's flight left later, giving them more time to spend before he left.

His mother cried once they got to the airport like she was never going to see her son again, and this bothered Kianne. She kissed her boys and gave her mom a couple of dollars. As they watched them all pass through security, Kianne was excited to get back to enjoying Vegas with his mom was not there to interfere.

James, Kianne and her dad went back to their room. They ordered breakfast and I grabbed a couple of shots from the fridge. Afterwards they headed to the strip. James bought his new father in law a 24-ounce cup of gin. With his bad hip, he strolled the strip, enjoying the little time he had left with his baby girl. With his son-n-law continuing to get him drunk, Kianne was getting worried he wouldn't be able to board the plane. It was 3:45 pm and her dad was a little on the wasted side. They took him back to their room so he could sleep of the liquor.

Sneaking down to the casino as he slept. James aggressively attached the poker table once again— as Kianne went to the slot machines. She wasn't big on gambling but played while her husband made enemies with the poker table. As she grabbed the waiter, Kianne just happened to see two white men suited up and sticking out like a sore thumb. She ordered a drink and anxiously waited. Before the waiter could hand her the drink, Kianne was reaching for it. Rushing to James. She kissed him on the neck and 'told him they had to go now. James tried to brush her off, but she stressed she wasn't feeling good and needed to go. Irritated, James got up, and Kianne walked him toward the men. They must have known what she was up to because they turned and parted ways, walking in different directions. As they got on the elevator, she told James what she had been seeing. First the one guy in the suit while she was shopping, then the two down in the casino area. He felt she was exaggerating. So, Kianne left it alone.

Getting back to the room, they grabbed her dad and headed to the airport. He sobered up a little, just enough to board the plane. They said their goodbyes and watched him get through security. Back at the hotel James and Kianne cuddled on the couch and ordered some food and a movie. Not sure when she dozed off, but of course Kianne woke up to an empty room again. James and poker were working her last nerves. She got up and headed downstairs and found him at another poker table. After his game, they went to walk the strip. They had three more days and were sure to enjoy them.

James and Kianne grabbed drinks, stopped in a couple small casinos and played some slots. They did some more shopping and relaxed by the pool for the rest of their trip. It was the first time they had been able to enjoy each other. Leaving Vegas well rested and at peace. That was until they made it back to Minnesota. Leaving the airport, taking a shuttle to Kianne's truck. There were five guys in suits. This old white man making conversation just happened to ask one of the men what he did for a living. The guy in the suit laughed as he said, "My boss is going to kill me, but I am a federal agent."

That's when I poked James and said, "I parked my truck here." We got off, not knowing where the truck was. I asked him, "Now do you believe me about the men in suits?" James shook his head in disbelief. This confirmed that they were watching him. Walking around the parking ramp, they finally found her truck. As they left the park and fly ramp and turned to get onto highway 494, Kianne gaslight came on. James gave her a look of death. It drove him crazy that she waited until the last minute to put gas in her truck. Driving west on Highway 494, she exited on 12th Avenue south and pulled into the Super America Express. James got out and pumped the gas. One thing she loved about him; he did things without her asking. He filled the tank up and they were back on the highway. Kianne drove north, exiting on Dowling Avenue fifteen minutes later, heading to now their home off 40th Avenue and Russell.

She pulled up in front the small brick house. James walked through the kitchen door first, turning off the alarm; they headed downstairs to their bedroom. As James went to turn the light switch on, his younger two children, Jhona and Ray, along with Black yelled out, "Congratulations!" Black had came over and cooked dinner with the kids to congratulate them on their marriage. We sat at the table in the family room and ate dinner. All the while James told the kids how my sixth sense was working overtime and the feds were all over Vegas. We shared what pictures were appropriate to share and called it a night.

.

~Running Water~

So much has happened in such a short time. Kianne was ready to get away from all the drama and deceitful friends her husband became accustomed to. Now she could admit, her so-called friends weren't too welcoming with her life decisions either. Yet she didn't live for them and gave a shit about what they had to say. Kianne have been pushing for them to move out-of-state the moment she said I do. After nagging James for the past two months, he finally put in the request for a transfer with his Parole Officer. No one knew they were planning this movie besides the Parole Officer and the attorney. They hadn't even told the kids. But in the meantime, Kianne began to look for houses outside of the cities. She didn't like the fact that James had so much traffic coming and going. She's never been one to have a lot of company in her house and she needed to put a stop to it. Kianne wasn't sure when or how but as they waited for the approval to move out of town, she became sick. One afternoon she was in so much pain lying in the bed, James walked in and cuddled with her. Not sure how long they were asleep; James woke up to several missed phone calls from Jase and Nick, his nephew. Mumbling to himself, asking how he didn't hear his phone—he dialed his nephew's number.

"What's up, nephew?"

"Aye Unc, did you speak to Jase? I think you need to go see about him."

"Is he good?"

"Naw! Ummm… just hit him up."

"All right cool, cool. I'll hit him up. Come on babe, let's go grab something to eat."

Kianne rolled out of the bed and trudged to the bathroom to fix herself up, then met James outside. As they were getting in the car, Savon pulled up on the side of James like a genie. He appeared as if he was notified whenever they were going out to eat.

"Yo Bro, what's good? Where we heading?"

"Taking my wife to eat, you are rolling?"

"Of course."

This irritated Kianne. It seemed that every time they mentioned food or thought of food this ass came around. It never failed. One day he would regret always inviting people to tag along. She prayed James stop the freeloading.

As they pulled into the Olive Garden parking lot in Saint Louis Park. The fat girl that lived inside Kianna already knew what to order and was just hoping she could keep it down. As soon as they walked in, the waitress escorted them toward the back of the restaurant. They ordered drinks then looked over the menu. Moments later Jase strolled in.

"Hey man, what's up? Did your nephew tell you I got picked up? Man, they picked me up this morning heading into town in a traffic stop; they were all over me."

"Is that right?"

"Man, they're coming for us. While I was being questioned, they had all these pictures, asking me who was who. They pointed to a picture of you, asking what your name was. The police asked if I knew you and told me you're not going anywhere. If you think you're moving to Louisiana, you have another think coming."

As soon as Jase mentioned the word "move", Kianne focused on their conversation. Since they never told anyone they were moving out of town. Let alone moving to Louisiana. James sat there calmly. Savon just watched and listened. When Jase had been interviewed by law enforcement, he was shown several photographs of potential participants. He admitted that he knew the individuals, including James. In the beginning Jase was denying any involvement in the federal investigation; until he was played a phone call where he spoke to another individual asking about a "bird". He then admitted to being involved for a short period.

"Man, they know," Jase stated in a panic. The waitress came back and took their order.

"I'm clean. So I'm not sure what you're talking about they coming so they had nothing on him. Jase replied, "They know." Kianne was so tired of hearing all the mess. If they knew anything, it was because he told. She was glad the food came. They all ate, and their conversation shifted elsewhere.

Savon talked about a transportation business. rolled my eyes because it was just something to bring up to ask for some money. James wasn't anything but an ATM to them all. Knowing him, I'm sure he would help a "fellow" friend— anything James thought that would make more money and put someone to work. But I knew it was bullish. I smelled it as soon as he opened his mouth.

They finished eating and Jase dipped out first. James, Kianne and Savon followed behind. Not one of them niggas attempted to put on the bill. Why should they? It irritated Kianne soul and one day she prayed he would see it! After hearing what Jase had to say; Kianne gut told her they should hold off on moving. Knowing that there was a case being established around James; she craved to tell James they should stay in Minnesota. But the attorney urged that they move; that it was for the best. When in reality, it was a means for the attorney to allow the feds to strategize their case.

~Transferred ~

James parole officer called the morning of November first. Delivering the news that his relocation was approved. Excited and scared at the same time—Kianne jumped out of bed to make a list of things to do. They told James to come in on November 3rd to discuss further instructions. It was odd they approved it so soon, knowing they were investigating him. Unless the conversation he had with Jase was more about himself and making it seem as if James was involved.

The morning he had to check in for his transfer. He parked in the lot off South 3rd street and 3rd avenue South. Checking his surroundings, he notices some familiar vehicles.

Kianne sitting in the passenger seat noticed James demeanor had changed. Looking around, she had seen the unmarked police cars. She got a funny feeling about James meeting. He went in to speak to his parole officer and sign some papers. Coming out he rushed to the car. Not wanting to be around all them Federal agents.

Eager to leave, Kianne helped her husband pack his things. Early that morning, they hit the road. James nephew and his friend were riding along to help drive. It was about 3 am when they pulled off. Curling up with a pink blanket, James grabbed his wife's hand, as she laid on his lap, they drove down I-94. Yet before they could get well into the trip, the trailer attached to the avalanche wheel busted.

Making it to Ames, Iowa—they stopped at a Menards to get the wheel fixed. An hour later stopping at a Kum -N - Go to gas up and grab some snacks—they continued their drive to Dallas, Texas. Riding with James was worse than riding with the kids. Every few hours they were stopping, and it drove Kianne crazy. Blindsided about the move. Kianne woke up to James pulling into his mom's driveway. He had dropped his nephew'nem off at his sister's house. Kianne thought about throwing a tantrum—she let it go. Since they were only staying the night—Kianne felt she could handle it.

James unpacked his bags, and they headed into the house. James stayed to talk with his mother, while Kianne went to bed.

Kianne woke up drenching wet in sweat—next to her James laid on his back snoring. She checked the time on her cell, it was three in the afternoon. She kissed James on the lips to wake him up. He rolled over, kissing her nipples. Kianne climbed on top and slid her honey stick inside. She leaned forward and slid her tongue in his mouth. They kissed to the rhythm of her hips. He palmed her ass cheeks and squeezed them together. Feeling her honey stick expanding as if he was about to explode. Kianne slowed down, planted soft pecks on his luscious lips. The moans he sang were music to her ears. She threw her head back and caught the wave. But he had other plans. James grabbed her hips, thrusting deep inside her. Before she could match his speed—James had flipped her over, his hand on the back of her neck pinned down. Kianne was about to come, but she heard his mother's voice whispering to Joe, *"They're in there making me a grandbaby."* Falling to her stomach, James followed as he came. She was completely turned off and disgusted. They both climbed out of bed to take a shower. Quarreling over the water. Kianne knelt under the water for round two. *"He will pay for my weave,"* she thought. He placed one palm on the shower wall and lean his head back in amazement. Once Kianne finished snatching his soul. They washed each other and stepped out the shower. They got dressed, and then joined his mom and dad in the living room. It wasn't long before Kianne nodded off during their conversation.

Waking up in the bed by herself. It was four in the morning. Kianne laid there with her eyes closed. Several minutes later James came in. He was loading the Cadillac so they could head toward Dallas. Over excited, Kianne got dressed and was in the car in a matter of seconds. They said their goodbyes to his parent and pulled off in to the morning traffic. Sitting in the passenger seat surfing the Internet. Kianne booking a hotel room near the Galleria, as James got on Highway 20 heading west. Two hours into the ride, he called his sister Sharon and told her they were on the way.

***

Five hours later, James pulled into a driveway to a brick house. He woke Kianne up before getting out of the car. As they strolled into the house—as soon as Sharon, James sister spoke out, "Hey Sis-n-law." Kianne knew they would bond. Her mouth filled with shiny gold adding to her already animated self. *"You must have kryptonite in your pussy?"* How in the hell you snatch my brother's last name?" In complete shocked of her words. *"The power of the tongue."* Kianne spit back, matching her vibe. James jumped in telling everybody to get in the car.

Sharon got in her car and followed them to the Hilton on Lyndon B. Johnson Freeway. James checks into their room and they all headed to get some food. He wanted to spend some time with his nieces and nephews. So killing two birds at once, James searched the nearest bowling alley. Kianne wasn't in the mood to do anything but eat and shop. She sat her skinny fat ass down, ordering wings and a bacon cheeseburger. James and the kids bowled—while Sharon and Kianne got to know each other.

After James whooped the kids in a couple of games in bowling. They said their goodbyes and headed back to the hotel. They had one more day before Kianne had to get back home. And she wanted to make sure she got as much alone time with her husband. The thought of being away for weeks was sickening.

Back at their room, Kianne ran some bath water and turned Pandora on. James sat on the bed looking into his phone. She walked in front of him and began to strip. A flirtatious smile appeared on his face. Motioning for him to follow with a finger, Kianne walked backward to the bathroom.

~Ex-Factor~

Shaniqua:

(n.) a common name used to mock/describe a Black woman from the inner city...this name would include all of the stereotypes: long fake braids, long colorful nails, ghetto voice, wears extremely tight and short clothing topped off with ridiculously long heels, and multiple children with different fathers.

http://www.urbandictionary.com/define.php?term=shaniqua

James had been gone for two weeks and it had been killing Kianne. To keep her mind off his absence. Kianne was heading out for her last girl's night out with family and friends. As she walked out the door, her phone chimed, "There goes my babe." Kianne answered the phone with a smile that could light up a Christmas tree. "Hey babe, what's up?"

"Nothing, packing and getting ready to head your way."

"I sure can't wait to see you!"

"Yeah, I know. Are you picking me up? Or should I get a cab?"

"Of course, I'm coming—why wouldn't I? Plus, you have my new baby. Well, you say you do. Do you?"

"Is that all you're worried about?"

"Well, yes." she laughed out loud. Kianne had been bugging him for a month about a dog—a teacup Yorkie that only gets up to three pounds. She was having baby fever but didn't want to give up her freedom yet. As she got into the car, Kianne notices a car in the shadows that was never there. The neighbors to the right of their house usually parked in their garage. To see a vehicle parked in their driveway was strange.

She shook it off and got in her truck. James asked where she was heading. "To the casino for a ladies' night," Kianne stated. He told her to drive safe, and he'd call in the morning on his way to the airport. Backing out the driveway, she pulled off down the alley. Turning up her music—letting Plies put me into a party fringe. Cruising down highway 94, her cousin called to check to see where she was. Kianne was twenty minutes away. She told them she would be there soon.

Kianne pulled in front of the casino and valet-parked her truck. Ready to gamble with her twenty dollar spending limit, she headed inside to find her girls. They had so much catching up to do. It was like she hadn't seen them in years. They walked around the casino chitchatting. All while playing random slots then headed up to the room they had before bingo started. Kianne was enjoying herself so much, she lost track of time. When she checked the time, it was 3 am. It was time for her to leave—she had to pick James up from the airport in a few hours.

The roads were horrible. Slipping and sliding down the

highway, Kianne drove as slowly as she could. She watched the other cars spin out of control. "Y'all out here speeding in this weather—as if you will get to your destination any faster. Let alone safe," she thought to herself. It took Kianne two hours to get home. Thinking she should have gone straight to the airport. She parked in the back and checked her surroundings. The dark vehicle two houses over was still there. Kianne called her husband to tell him. It didn't look like the police, but it worried her—he had many enemies. He answered as if he was up partying. She made a mental note for later. Her focus was on the vehicle. "Bae, I've been seeing this car around the house. I don't think it's the police."

"Okay, be cool and lock up the house—set the alarm and be prepared. Keep your phone close in case you have to call the police."

"Ok love." They spoke briefly about his flight before ending the call. Glad he talked her into getting her license to carry. She grabbed her peacemaker out the safe—unlocked it, loaded it up and placed it on the bathroom towel rack. She took a quick shower. Before getting in bed she took her protector for the night, placing it on the headboard and dozed off.

The piercing sound from the alarm clock scared the crap

out of Kianne. Three hours of sleep wasn't enough. It was eight in the morning, Kianne rolled over smiling, knowing her husband was landing soon. She turned the news on to catch the weather. The roads were horrible last night. She knew flights would have many delays. James's flight was to land at 10 am. While she got herself together, her phone rang. It was the movers calling to tell her they were running three hours late. As she ended the call, she grabbed her keys and purse and left for the airport. The roads were not cleared—once again the state was slow on their job. Kianne was driving about 45 mph on the highway with few cars on the road. A 25-minute drive took 40 minutes. Kianne parked the truck and went inside to wait. She walked to the display to see if James plane had landed, her phone sang out, "There goes my babe." She smiled from the inside out. "Where are you?" James spoke through the phone.

"In the airport, sitting by the display screen. Where are you?"

"I'm getting my bags at baggage claim number 8."

"Ok, here I come." Walking through the crowd toward my babe, I got excited all over again. It felt like I hadn't seen him in years. I spotted him with his bag—waved at him and smiled. He gave me a grin and walked out of the exit door.

Following suit, I walked out the nearest entrance. Stepping into the crisp air, I stood with my head down, twirling my thumbs. Glancing out of the corner of my eye, I saw my babe walk toward me slowly, like he was trying to come up with a line to impress me. I laughed to myself. He approached me and stood there. Leaned over and whispered in my ear, "Excuse me, miss, but you are one beautiful woman." Kianne grin from ear to ear, "Thank you

"This may be a bit much, but can I take you to lunch? And before you say no, let me show you something." In his right hand was a case with his blanket laying over it. Kianne paid no attention to it. He opened it, reaching inside, he pulled out this little black dog the size of his hand. "You got the dog!"

"Of course, I did, for my Angel." Kianne pulled the puppy to her chest and cuddled with her, grabbing her husband's hand. She leaned up and gave him a kiss and they left the airport.

James and Kianne made it home as the movers called to let them know they were thirty minutes away. Kianne rushed her dog inside the house because she was shivering. Letting her go in her new home. Kianne led James to the bedroom— pushed him down on the bed and straddled him.

"We've got about 20 minutes before the movers get here." Kianne giggled. With a grin, he flipped his wife over and placed his lips close to hers.

"Come on, love, you know I can do a lot in thirty minutes."

***

Kianne phone rang, she reached over to answer it. The movers were outside. Kianne got in the shower and James open the door for them. The movers came in, looked throughout the house and started to pack the living room. Kianne got dressed and sat at the bar where she found James. He was on the phone with someone. She grabbed the dog and placed her on the bar table. Thinking of a name to name her. James hung up the phone and kissed his wife.

"I am glad we are getting out of here."

"You and me both." she reached over to grab him a beer from the fridge. With her butt in the air, he slapped it.

"Don't start nothing you can't finish, Mr. Fields.

"You trying to go another round?"

"I'm saying, thirty minutes wasn't enough."

"Oh, you trying to make a baby?"

"Honey, that's why you purchased the dog—That's it! Her name is Honey." James smiled and said it fits. In the midst of their conversation—Kianne saw a shadow appeared from behind the wall of the basement stairwell. As if a ghost entered the room.

"I can't believe the shit I'm seeing. This bitch bold as hell." James' ex-bitch strutted in the house as she lived there. Tall bobble-headed, bug-eyed, skinny hoe walked in the house and invaded their space. Kianne jumped up off the bar stool, ready to whoop her ass. Taking one step, Kianne felt her weight go and cascaded to the floor. James pushed her aside into the stacked boxes that were against the wall. As she slid to the floor, James grabs Shaniqua by the neck, manhandling her up the stairs. Through clenched teeth, he hissed, "Bitch, you done lost your mind. What the fuck you doing walking in my house?" Shaniqua scuffled back and dug her heels at the doorway.

"You were supposed to love me! You said you would never leave me and you over here playing house with your wife. You didn't tell anybody you were moving out of town."

James held her in one clenched fist and opened the screen door as he shoved her outside. "What the fuck is wrong with you? We been over." Kianne was at the screen door. Out on the street she recognized a black sedan. Inside, one of James' girls was behind the wheel. She seemed to be enjoying the show.

"That's why we phucked last week."

"Bet you lying," Kianne screamed—goofy bitch. Tricks are for kids and he has enough of those, hoe!"

"What the fuck wrong with you," James questioned. She didn't have half the senses God gave a billy goat. James stood in front of the door, blocking Kianne. Shaniqua stood in the neighbor's yard between their houses. The front yard was an ice field from the passing storm—hoping she slide and bust her head open. Her car parked in the neighbor's drive way with her youngest son in his car seat. Heading to the front door, Kianne I was tired of acting like a lady—this time he would not stop her from choking her ass out. Shaniqua had gotten the last laugh from following us to dinner a few weeks back. Ole stalking hoe.

Kianne swung the front door open—to her surprise, Savon was standing in front of the door. "Baby girl, I can't let you out." Kianne could spit fire. "Ain't this a bitch!" She ran to the kitchen door. James was still guarding it, arguing with the bitch.

"Let her out!" Shaniqua called out. Still standing in the neighbor's yard, with a fence blocking her. Kianne raised her .380 Smith and Wesson to the side of her head—using her thumb to scratch the side of her face. Shaniqua's face turned white as a ghost. At this point, James leaped toward her. She screamed, "Hit me then, hit me, James. That's what you want to do."

Kianne shook her head. This girl was freaking nuts. James picked up a brick—raising it as if he was about to throw it at her car. She ran to her car screaming, "My baby is in there- my baby is in there." She jumped inside and sped off. All this drama was the reason Kianne was ready to move. Kianne apologized to the movers, then went down stairs and laid down on the bed. James followed and lay next to her.

"Babe, I am sorry!" Kianne ignored him. Tired of the bullshit, **beneth**

she knew how the bitch found out and so did he.

***

Once the movers finally got the house packed and, on the truck, they left to deliver their things to storage. While Kianne and the boys went to a hotel. James had some things to handle before they left town.

James made it to the hotel early morning. Kianne wanted to snap about his ex popping up but was too tired. She was trying not to be the nagging wife. Four hours later, Kianne rolled over to James sitting up at the edge of the bed talking on the phone. She hated that phone. She went to check on the boys and started to pack some of their things, so James could load the truck. Kianne wanted to leave before the snowstorm Minnesota was calling for came. They made several stops, said their goodbyes and headed south on Highway 35W.

Kianne rubbed her tired eyes. Eager to escape Minnesota, three hours into driving, she was drained. She took the next exit for a gas station to get a Energy drink. James took the boys to the bathroom and walked Honey. James' phone rang and Kianne peeked at the screen. She didn't recognize the number, so she let it go to voice mail. The thoughts of Jase speaking to the Feds had filled her head. As she was sitting in her thoughts, the boys and James got back in the truck and they pulled off.

"Bae, what if that attorney told you to move so the Feds can build a case around you? They spoke with Jase and he's not in jail. You don't' find it funny?"

"Black isn't either, but I know they were following him. Them people have nothing on me." "Well, I hope you're right." Kianne finished the rest of her Energy drink—turned up the volume and let Heather Headley caress her ears as she took the road to a new beginning.

~Something New~

Moving to Karen's house once they made it to Monroe was not part of the discussion Kianne and James had. What Kianne do recall was discussing their move to Dallas, TX. Yet, sixteen hours later, on Thanksgiving morning, here they were pulling into the Comfort Suites off Martin Luther King Jr. Drive in Monroe, LA. James mom was in Mississippi visiting Joe's family. Sitting in the car waiting for James to check into the rooms, his phone vibrated. Kianne leaned over and saw the name Nia. The devil crept inside, and the pits of hell rested in her soul. She opened the message and deleted it. James came walking out with the keys. They then drove around to the back, entering through the hotel back door to unload their bags. Kianne took a shower and grabbed a couple of dollars and headed to the closest liquor store. James and the boys went over to his sister's house. Back at the hotel—Kianne was tired from doing most of the driving and irritated from what she had read.

Sipping a glass of Nuvo, lying across the bed, Kianne peace didn't last long. James came back with his nephews to go swimming. At this time, she was unaware of the issues they would have with his family constantly wanting to be around.

The next morning his mom and pop returned from Mississippi. She broke the news of not moving to Dallas when she drove Kianne's truck to pick her up from the hotel. That explained the text James sent about checking out and why he took their bags when he left. Another thing that irritated Kianne, James allowing anyone to just grab car keys and drive off. Refusing to live under that woman's roof. Kianne searched on Craigslist, and after coming up with shit. She decided to drive around town and look for a place to live. Dropping his mom off at her house, she drove off. She drove for hours, coming up with nothing—Kianne stopped at Red Lobster to grab some food. Taking a seat in a booth at the back of the restaurant, she ordered the Ultimate Feast and a glass of Pinot Grigio. Just as the waiter walked away from taking the order, James called telling her to meet him at the address he texted. Two glasses of wine later, Kianne left and headed to the address she was sent. When she pulled up into a small shopping center parking lot. There were several stores, including a strip club on the far-left end from where James was parked. Rolling her eyes, Kianne got out of the truck as James came to a glass door to a store front. "What do you think?"

"Of what?" she stated with an attitude.

"The store. We're opening a cell phone store."

"What the hell? Why would you go and do that?"

"Open a family business?"

"You opened a store without discussing it with me for one. And on top of that, this is an extremely large purchase."

Taking it upon himself to open a cell phone store and have his nephews work there. Kianne knew deep down this was a bad idea. Being the wife she was, she stayed in her place. His money, his problems.

James introduced Kianne to a guy named Dre, another

ex-con, which meant another snake. All Kianne cared about was making sure money was accounted for. Leaving James to his new project. Kianne went to his mom's house. The boys were sleep, so Kianne got in the shower and crawled in the bed. Lying there, a voice whispered to her, or was it her woman's intuition? The little voice spoke loudly when it said to pick up his mama's phone and look through the call history. And look here, that bobble—head's number was listed, one too many damn times for Kianne. Her wondering thoughts were accurate. Her blood was boiling, and spirit was screaming. Kianne started to drive to the store but decided to hold on to the information. Instead, she got dressed and drove to the drive-in bar and ordered a 32-ounce Long Island ice tea. Sipping her tea, Kianne drove around the small town, as if she was in a Freddy Krueger movie. Several hours into the nightmare, she found myself on Forsythe Avenue. Passing Neville High School, a house with a "for rent" sign in the yard at 1010 Forsythe Avenue, three-bedroom, two-bathroom, single family house. Great for their soon-to-be growing family. Kianne said a small prayer in her head asking God that he gave it to them. Then drove back to the house. Pulling up, she saw the Suburban parked. Checking her phone; it was 3:28 am. Smiling from the inside out, Kianne pulled off and headed to the Walmart in West Monroe.

Skipping towards the aisle with the men's body spray. She grabbed a bottle of Old Spice and sprayed it in the air, then walked through the mist. With a grin, she left and drove back to the house. Parking her X5 on the side of the Suburban, Kianne pranced in the house, feeling all bubbly inside. The house was quiet, dark with a stream of light coming from the kitchen window. Walking into the bedroom, James was sitting on the edge of the bed plastered, looking into his phone. He had a malicious look on his face when he glanced up. "You think this shit is cool?" James' eyes were beady black dots with a red glaze. Kianne walked in the room attempting pass him. That Old Spice must had hit his nostrils because she didn't make it past his right knee before he grabbed her by the arm and flung her on the bed. She tried to hold a laugh, but it came out. Kianne had hit a nerve. Smiling within and scooting away, she stripped then climbed into the bed naked. James leaned over and tried to grab a titty. Smacking his hand, she told him to call that bobble-headed bitch. Then rolled over and went to sleep.

***

Kianne woke up with a slight headache as she laid next to her hubby until his snoring came to a halt. Once James woke up, she told him about the house and rushed him to get ready, so they could ride back over there. Driving to the house she found in the wee hours. A lady was in the front yard as they pulled into the driveway. James introduced themselves, then asked if they could look at the house. As he proceeds to ask questions about the house. Kianne took in how beautiful it was. The house had three bedrooms, two baths, a family room, a formal dining room with a fireplace in the living room and a extremely large back yard. It was extremely dusty, as if no one had lived there for years. Nothing some bleach and Lysol couldn't fix. It was better than living with his mother. She offered to lease the home right then and there. James paid the rent and damage deposit. She handed Kianne the keys to their new home. Later that evening she called the movers to have the furniture delivered from storage. After being told it would take a week. She made reservations at the hotel. Kianne refused to stay at her mother n law's till then.

The day of the move, Kianne met the movers at the new house. As they unloaded the truck, the boxes were wet, and you could tell they searched through their belongings. A tv was broke and the furniture legs were missing. The movers advised her to file an insurance claim.

Weeks had gone by—taking a step back, for once things

seemed normal. Kianne was glad to be starting their new life. Yet forgetting their actual lifestyle, they were becoming too comfortable. One morning while James took the boys to school as normal. Walking out the front door, across the street there was a church, and parked in the parking lot was a charcoal charger. Without a doubt, the feds were watching. He went ahead and dropped the boys off at school. After seeing the FEDS parked out front. James was ready to move.

~New Edition~

While Kianne was packing some things up and getting dinner out to cook. James had dropped the boys off from school and was headed back to his store. Kianne truly despised of it. Knowing it was a bad investment. Sitting down folding clothes it dawned on her that she never had a period. "Oh shit," trying to do the math in her head. Kianne got up and told the boys she was heading to the store. As she drove to CVS, thinking about purchasing the whole row of pregnancy test. Kianne got back home and took one of the three pregnancy tests that she purchased. The first one stated positive. A river of tears rolled down her face. Kianne wanted to wait due to everything that was going on. She took the second test. Positive. Laughing out loud, walking out the bathroom the boys looked at their mother crazy. She went to their bedroom and place the two tests on the nightstand and sat on the edge of the bed. Pulling at the little bit of hair she had on her head, Kianne cried. In complete shock, Kianne thought about the few times she took a Plan B. Drinking the glass of water sitting on the nightstand and twenty minutes later Kianne took the third and final test. Fucking positive. Calling her husband to ask how soon he will be home. She went to the kitchen to pour him a glass of black Hennessy and place it next to the three test she just took. Filled with so many emotions. *I ask for a dog, Honey,* thinking to herself. *I wanted to enjoy our marriage.* In spite of all that was going on, that wasn't going to be the case. James walked in the door screaming "baby where you at?" Instead of coming to the one room I had privacy at since he always had people in the house, I ignored his call. "Baby" he screams louder as he walked down the hallway to our bedroom. "You hear me calling!"

"I didn't hear you call out Kianne." I was one of the strange ones who despised of being called pet names. No telling how many women he called babe before me. I hated it.

"Funny. What are you doing?"

"I was thinking about the test I failed."

"Huh, I thought school was out for winter break?"

"No, the tests that are on the nightstand."

"What did you cook for dinner?"

"Yea, about that, I didn't get a chance to get it done."
"You mean to tell me that you been here all damn day and there's no dinner ready? What have the boys ate?" As if she was invisible, Kianne stood there. So many thoughts running through her head. Smiling, "there's a glass of Henny Black on the night stand." She left her husband standing there and went to see what the boys wanted for dinner.

"WHAT THE HELlo" Kianne. James came full speed out the room. "Are you sure? Is this real? I thought you wanted to wait?"

"I did. This wasn't in the plan. We have so much shit going on. We don't even know if or when you will be leaving us."

Grabbing her by the waist, James wrapped Kianne in his arms. Their marriage was becoming more of a movie than a union created before God. James kissed his wife on the forehead and they all headed to Olive Garden to eat.

Being in Monroe with no family and friends. Kianne had to call the one person she didn't want too. Her sister n law Monique. Asking for help to find a good clinic. After the many questions her nosy ass asked, she finally gave the information to the clinic she attended. Although Kianne advised her that she didn't need the company. Her and her daughter n law met Kianne and stayed in the clinic lobby. After answering basic questions and taking a test, they came back with what Kianne already knew. She was pregnant.

***

Once again, Kianne was on the search for a new house. Not sure if the Feds threw the house at her but after several days of searching craigslist. She found what could have been her dream home in Monroe LA. Located at 2214 Emerson street, there was three bed rooms two bathrooms, and a mother in law suite. Falling in love with the open floor length windows, the modern style kitchen and the oversized master bath tub; which was brand new. They weren't in the first place for more than a month. Kianne called the rental manager and advised her of their vacating. James paid a thousand dollars to hold the property. Then there was a closing set up. It was weird since it was a rent to purchase. The owner was asking for a fifth-teen thousand dollar down payment. James had the funds wired from his accountant. When they got to the office there were four people in the room. The owner of the house, the realtor, the assistant and a man who the realtor introduced as his lawyer friend. The realtor told us the wire never came through. James offered to bring cash in. With a clouded judgment and wanting the house. Kianne ignored all signs that day. James and Kianne went to the bank, the store and the house to grab what money was on hand. Counting fifth-teen thousand dollars 4 times before they walked out the house. Handing the funds to the assistant, she came back telling them it was one dollar short. Bullshit. *"I know what I counted."* The realtor laughed and said that's okay. Once again too comfortable and blind by the lifestyle, needing to have that big house. After signing the lease and getting the keys from the owner. They went home to move into their new house.

~The-Invasion~

Sitting in the office, James sat looking out the office window. Admiring the body of his wife—as her gracefulness moved around getting the store running up to speed. His phone rang. The screen showed an unknown number. For a minute he thought not to answer it, thinking it was that ole girl from Minnesota. Curious to know, he answered it. On the other end of the line was his brotha. The one that he had love for, would die for and even disappoint his wife for. was calling. Knowing that the Feds had recently picked him, James was helping pay for his legal fees. Even after Kianne advised him not too. Blinded by trust and loyalty, something that he did not realize many lack within themselves. A woman's instinct was unexplainable, because Kianne knew that every one of them was out for themselves. He answered the call and listened to his homie throw demands at me. Thinking to himself, "Black has his own money and the Feds didn't take it, nor was he working for me when I was in the streets." Any help that James provided was out of love. But he was working his number and robbing him at the same time. Black was trying to get all that he could before they arrested James. Knowing he betrayed James to save himself. Finishing the call, James tapped on the glass to signal his wife to come in the office. He had to break the bad news and explain how he assisted Black with his legal matters.

Kianne walked into the office, the look in his eyes told her it wasn't good. "Babe, Black called. He got picked up."

"James, Black's going to tell. Ain't no nigga about to do time at the age to 40 for no one!" Kianne tried to warn. Her gut wanted to say let's move back to Minnesota or better yet run to Mexico. James explained how Black demanded that he pay for his attorney fees. *"James give Black the money he paid for the truck."* Deep down Kianne knew James already paid his attorney fees. You can't tell a person that knows it all anything. *"Babe, it's too late.* I already gave him the money plus more."

Furious at James actions, Kianne needed to get ready to go to Minnesota to move her mother. Not wanting to leave the boys and James home alone at this point. Scared that the Feds would come and snatch him while she was away. Before Kianne left the store, she asked James' cousin to keep an eye out on him. As she got in the truck, James' phone vibrated. Kianne looked down and saw the name Nia. He quickly hit the side button and ignored the call. She made a mental note to check that phone when she got in the house. She wasn't in the mood to fight or catch a case. After pulling out her 380 on some thirsty bitch the other day, she was over fighting with him.

They had to be up at 4:30 am to drop Kianne off at the airport. Her flight was scheduled to leave at 6 am. Heading to Minnesota to move her mom to South Carolina. Everything was packed. All she needed to do was get there and drive the truck back. Knowing her husband, he would be needing a babysitter more than the boys. Something told her he would be in some trouble. The dream she had days ago of four dead bodies on their lawn worried her.

Arriving in Minnesota, the first stop was to Chipotle. Kianne was deprived and being reunited with the famous burrito place was exciting. Then she headed over to the U-Haul place to pick up the truck. And of course, the rental was screwed up. They only had a 10-foot truck left and they had to move a two-bedroom apartment. Not having a choice, Kianne took the small truck and headed to her mom's in Shoreview to load up. By 11 pm the truck was load and they were on the road. Crossing the Hudson bridge, it wasn't long before Kianne got on the highway heading East on 94 when James called. "Babe, I just got shot at," James blurted out.

While driving, Kianne listened as he explained what took place back home. After the basketball game they dropped off the boys, then went to the strip club. Kianne specifically stated to stay away from. Leaving the club James seen Dre breaking up a fight. Not thinking much of it, he drove home. "Babe, as I pulled up to the house and parked at the end of the driveway closer to the back yard, I jumped out to water the bushes. With my head leaned back, I heard a voice yell, *"Don't move."* I saw a guy pointing at gun. In a matter of seconds, I had to make a decision to either go in the house where the kids were or run from it." At that moment Kianne regretted feeding him so many home cooked meals. James ran to the right, heading toward the front of the house and across the street. The good thing about the neighborhood was that all the houses had tall bushes. Running between the two houses on the corner, he heard gun fire: POP–POP– POP... POP–POP. Those cats were amateurs—not one shot hit me." Kianne heard Don in the background. James continued to explain the events that took place. Mentioning that the police just left, and they were headed to a hotel. She knew something was going to happen. After hanging up the phone, Kianne told her mom what happened. It probably wasn't a good idea since she ran her mouth like water. Ready to get home, driving down I-94 east, all she could think of were her boys.

Nineteen hours later Kianne and her mom pulled into Bowman, South Carolina. Rushing out of the truck and into her granny's kitchen, on a mission to find a home cooked meal. As usual, there was eggs and rice with bacon sitting on the stove; that woman never failed. After fixing a plate, Kianne sat at the table and danced to the rhythm of her chewing. Food was comforting and once finished, she went into the open bedroom and passed out.

The next morning, Kianne woke up to the sound of a deep raspy voice yelling in the room. "Duck, you asleep?" her favorite uncle called out. Rolling out the bed and waddling to give him a hug. He was one of the main reasons why she was so spoiled. When her father left, he stepped in and helped raise her. He never told Kianne no. Whatever she wanted he provided. It was always special when the two seen each other. They went to Grandma's kitchen and sat down to eat some more. They talked about life and what Kianne was doing with hers. He asked about her new husband, making sure he was treating his niece right. Then he took her to the airport, so Kianne could get back to her family.

***

After making it home from the move. She crawled in their bed to let her body rest. Yet, it wasn't long after James had dropped her off that he was calling to tell her he invited his family for over dinner. He didn't bother to ask if she was up to cooking—just like a man. Kianne got out of bed and went to the grocery store. Rushing back home, she started to cook fried chicken and three-cheese scalloped potatoes with biscuits. Extremely tired, swollen feet, with a back that felt as if she was carrying the world on it was killing her. Kianne knew James was going to pay for this. By 6 pm James decided to stroll in the kitchen door with his Mom and Pop. Soon after his sister and husband scrolled in. Before she knew it, there were about twelve people at the dining room table. Kianne slid in James' lap as his sister ran her mouth a mile a minute, talking about how they were going to have 10 kids. Laughing out aloud, she thought to herself; *Yeah, I'll have ten kids in my throat.* The way this pregnancy was going, she was good on having any more kids. But it was nice to see James sit down with his family.

A little after midnight, everyone started to flee. The house became empty, the kids were in bed and Kianne was dead tired. After taking a much needed shower she crawled into the bed. James straightened up the kitchen, then join Kianne in bed. He laid at the end rubbing her swollen feet. Honey, their teacup Yorkie that slept by the bedroom door started to yap in a high pitch. James bolted up. Honey dashed to the kitchen door steady yapping. Kianne slide out the bed clutching her nine. Peeking thru the hallway window curtains, she made her way into the kitchen standing on the side of the doorway out of sight. As he stepped out of the shadows walking around the house. Kianne stood expecting some ignorant fuck to try it again. James came back in. Babe, he called out. Kianne tiptoed forward from the floor length curtains. "Oh shit, look at you!"

"Did you see anything?"

"No, nothing." They both spun to honey, she cocked her head sideways as if she said what the fuck ya'll looking at. I heard shit. They checked the windows and all six doors then went to bed. It wasn't long before Kianne drifted into her last peaceful sleep.

~I see you~

Thursday April 14th, 2011, 6 am. Their son Drew knocked on the door to let them know they were ready to get dropped off. James rolled over and said he'd take the boys to school this morning. Thankful for his consideration—after last night Kianne's body was done for the week. James got up, put on some sweats and drove the boys to school.

As he drove the boys to school, James notice a blacked-out Ford Taurus following him. With the school literally five minutes from the house. He cut a couple corners taking a longer route to get there. Drew was watching as James watched the rearview mirror. Right then he knew that they were picking him up today. He felt it and Drew felt it too. Kids may not know what's going on, but they know when things are bad. This all was crushing James inside. Just getting settled into the house, the new baby and the boys feeling comfortable with the move. James was kicking myself in the ass.

Pulling up to the school. He Parked the truck and called his wife. Handing Drew his wallet, he whispered to give it to his mom.

***

Before Kianne could doze back off, James called within minutes of leaving the house.

"Babe, they're here, I think they're picking me up today. I knew something was up when I started seeing all these unmarked cars and the random phone calls from strangers." Bae, I'm gonna let them just follow me around the city."

Kianne sprang up out of the bed like a jack-in-the-box. "No, come back home after you drop them off."

"Ok."

"Take the back way and drive slowly."

It was Drew's turn to bring snacks. James grabbed the bags of Capri Suns and two bags of individual chips, walked into the school. The agents followed behind as if he would run. *"Babe, if I go out this back door I can run for it."* It sounded good at the time. But who was he fooling? He was out of shape and overweight. Once again, Kianne regretted cooking daily and making him come home for dinner.

With panic in her voice, Kianne screamed *"No!* Just come home." Sitting on the edge of the bed asking a million and one questions, she jumped up and put on a pair of James' boxers and started to move around the house. It dawned on her that they would be roaming the house.

"What are you doing?" James blurted out. With the phone to her ear. Out of breath, she shouted, "What do you think? Getting rid of your toys!"

"Oh. OH, damn, I forgot. Ok, I just pulled off. I'll be pulling up in a few."

"Okay, two minutes please, just two minutes." Running through the house like a chicken with its head cut off. Kianne ran from the mother-in-law suite to the family room into the main hallway where the front door was and then the laundry room, grabbing every gun that was hid at the entryways. She ran outside frantic, not sure what to do or where to put them. Running to the back of the house, she threw the garbage bag

of guns into the neighbor's yard. Luckily there were leaves and it landed in a pile of them. As Kianne was walking back in the house, James pulled into the carport and rushed through the back door.

"Good looking, bae."

"Yeah, whatever! Shit! I'm tired."

~The Raid~

Standing in the kitchen, staring at her husband while he explained how the Monroe police were following him—the look on his face scared me. I knew today was the day!

"Baby, they followed me from the house to the school, in the school and back here. Look out the window, you see 'em parked at the second house there?"

"Yeah, bae. If they wanted you they would have come in, right? They would have pulled you over. Call the lawyer back and see what he says."

Looking across the kitchen at her husband, Kianne seen flashing lights. She ran toward him, yelling, "Bae, they're outside!" BOOM. "FREEZE! GET DOWN! GET DOWN!" They dropped to the floor—James begin to yell, *"My wife is pregnant— she can't get down all the way."* ATF swarmed the home, six entries with at least two to three men coming through each door. All they saw was guns and lights. Kianne thinking, This SHIT is crazy. All this for one man. Yelling for James to crawl towards one of the officers, another officer said into a radio, *"We have the suspects down."* Ordering them to their feet, they led them outside. Kianne couldn't believe all the cars they had just for her husband. An army tank was in the back yard. Standing outside as they searched and roamed through their house, Kianne thought the worst has come. They had talked about this many of times and she had mentally prepared myself for this day. But who would have thought that the things we spoke about were happening right before my eyes? After they searched James, he yelled, *"I love you, Babe"* then put him in a squad car and drove away.

Watching her husband be taken away, knowing this was the last time she would see him as a free man— Kianne's world crumbled into many pieces. The tears wanted to come, but her pride wouldn't allow her to show these people the hurt. The officers were walking around smiling, whispering like they hit the jackpot.

I never knew I would be going through this. I knew what I was getting into. The possibility of James doing jail. I guess

I never thought I would be dealing with it firsthand. I didn't believe that it would happen. I knew his family was praying I would leave. His mother had already made a call to his family in Minnesota, telling them not to help me financially. But if I were to leave him, what was the purpose of marrying this man? For better or worse, right? That's why I did it. I loved him for who he was. James came into my life and loved me for me. My kids fell in love with him. He gave them the attention young men needed, that father and son time, even when it was work around the house. They complained but the time spent was worth it. I knew what I was facing. I knew the type of man I had. God would see us through this. But still I didn't believe it all. How could you cook for your family one night and wake up to chaos?

They allowed Kianne to put some clothes on and brought her down to the Federal Holding department. Sitting in a small room next to her husband listening to their conversation. Asking all kinds of questions, playing audio tapes with his voice on them, telling him they knew what that meant.

As Kianne bent down on the floor with her ear to the heating vent, someone knocked on the door. Two white men walked in, introducing themselves as Detectives Jim and Jim. "James, huh? You know all James's think alike!"

"No, no, no. We're different from your James."

"So, you say."

"Well, we would like to ask you some questions about your husband James Earl Fields. But first we will ask a couple of questions about you."

"Yea, ok."

"What is your full name?"

"Kianne Fields."

"And you are legally married to James Earl Fields? How long have you guys been married?"

"Yes, seven months. But you guys know this already!"

"What is it that you do for a living?"

"I'm a hair stylist and James work at our cell phone store."

"Do you guys make decent money? The house you're in looks like a house on Lake Calhoun. It's huge; my house isn't that big."

"Am I under an arrest, Jim?"

"Oh no."

"Is my husband coming home with me today?"

They chucked. "No, not today."

"Well, I think I'm done talking to y'all."

"Well, you do know your husband is a dope dealer," the main officer growled through clenched teeth. "He doesn't move anything unless it makes him a million. We got him this time, and he's heading back to Minnesota to prison."

Kianne rolled her eyes, leaned back in the chair and studied the pimple-headed FBI agent. "Say what you want, but my baby is coming home," she thought. They had Kianne sitting in the room for about thirty more minutes. An officer came in to let her know a car was waiting to take her home.

When Kianne got home, those crooked ass cops were still roaming throughout her house. While she sat in the back of the police car, an officer came to the window asking about a man on a paper. 'Ummm, ma'am, do you know this person?"

"No."

"Are you sure? This is one of the men that tried to rob your husband."

"Oh really? Huh!"

"He is supposed to be your husband's cousin."

"Never seen him till now."

"Okay, well we should be done shortly."

I was glad he showed me that picture! I couldn't wait to talk to James. This shit was crazy. I had seen this entire situation coming but there wasn't anything I could have done to prevent it. I was getting tired of sitting in the back of the police car. My legs were cramping on me, and I was hungry.

What the hell were they looking for anyway? Wasn't shit in the house. If they had been watching him as they say. They would had known he don't shit where he lay!

One of the ATF agents came to the car and told her they were leaving, he mentioned that the keys were on the table in the house and she could go in. As Kianne walked in their house she could see they were pissed off. Whatever they were looking for was not here. The front door was busted open. The living room was turned upside down—pictures off the wall, couch pillows tossed. Kianne shook her head. The kitchen wasn't bad. They took the liberty of helping themselves. They drunk Kianne pop. *"Oh, hell no, they ate my cookies*—seriously, messing with a pregnant woman's food. Kianne walked towards the back. The air vents were off the hinges. *"What was that all about?"* Their room was a mess. All James shoes were out, and his clothes were everywhere. The safe was busted open. *"They could have just asked for the code."*

Kianne didn't understand why they had to go through their shit like this. As she sat on their bed—Kianne seen they took their time and went through their wedding book. Tears rolled down the side of her face as she thought about this morning's events. Her husband was heading to prison for an unknown amount of years. Kianne laid on the bed and cried, inhaling James scent from their sheets. She cried some more, until I cried myself to sleep.

The doorbell rang, and Kianne jumped up. Her mother and father-in-law walked in, asking if she was ok. She assured them that she was fine and wasn't hurt. They started to ask questions that Kianne didn't want to answer. She told them the main details anyway. Then asked them to take her to the store to get some paperwork.

When they arrived at the store, James sister Monique and her husband were pulling up as well. Kianne opened up the doors and they all went inside. Kianne looked around and notice some phones missing. Baby Fields got to kicking as her stress levels went up. She went to the office to sit. There were a lot of chattering going on in the front of the store. Kianne wasn't sure what the hell everyone was talking about, her mind was running wild. Monique was running her mouth a mile a minute. She mentioned something about Kianne posting pictures on Facebook. Kianne stepped to the office door. "This has nothing to do with any Facebook or anything with Monroe. You guys kill me, so miss me with all that nonsense about it's my fault." Kianne shook her head and went to sit back down in the office. Tears started to form in her eyes, a burning river flowed down her cheeks. In the mist of her thoughts, Karen walked in asking if she was okay. Then turned around and asked for twenty dollars. *"She never cease to amaze me,"* Kianne chuckled.

Kianne sat in the office trying to figure out what her next move would be. She heard James no-good, supposed-to-be nephew Blue walk in the store. The moment Kianne met him, she got bad vibes. She instantly went to see what he wanted.

Blue started asking everyone what happened. Kianne said nothing. She walked to the cell phone case with the missing Phones. Directing her question to Blue—"What happen to the phones?"

"Oh I took them out this Morning," Blue stuttered.

"Ok, you can bring them back now." Her nerves were already bad—she couldn't deal with people anymore. She made up her mind that she was closing the store and heading back to MN. There was no way she was staying down here with his family.

Kianne asked for a ride to get the boys from school. The had no idea that their dad was gone and wouldn't be coming back any time soon. How was she going to explain to them the events that took place today? She wanted to cry again but her pride wouldn't allow it. She picked the boys up and headed home to clean the mess they left— while waiting on her husband to call. She had no clue where he was and what to do.

Kianne laid on James side of the bed, inhaled his scent, hugged his pillow and cried. She felt her world being snatched from beneath her. While she laid in her room, the boys started to clean up the house.

The phone rang. Kianne jumped up and quickly answered it. *"You have a collect call from James Fields, an inmate in Bossier County Jail. To accept this call press 5."* Before the automatic message could finish Kianne was pressing the number 5.

"Babe, are you ok?"

"I'm fine. I can't believe this is all happening."

"I know, but I need you to grab a pen and write down everything I tell you. First, you need to call the lawyer, tell him I'm at Bossier County. Call fam and tell them you need help. Go find Red Son and tell him you need all that. Then have Dre sign all the paperwork to the store over to you." He was rambling off so much as she tried to keep up. Knowing their time was short with the county calls. "What do you want to do?"

"I want to be wherever they're taking you."

"Well, they shipping me back to Minnesota, so start

looking for a place and decide when you leaving. Call Ray and have him come help you move— *Man this is crazy babe, I miss you all ready.*"

"Yeah, who you telling. You know they took all the cars, knocked down the back fence and tore up the house, went in heating vents, pulled all your clothes out, took all the paperwork on the cars, kids, and my credit cards, and left me with $30."

"You have one-minute left," the automatic lady voice blasted.

"Babe, I love you and I want to assure you everything will be all right."

"I love you too, and I'm praying for us."

The phone hung up. I believed every word that came through my phone. I rubbed my belly as our baby boy begin to kick. I knew I was doing too much. I set the phone and notebook down beside me and laid down. I needed to rest for a little bit before making those phone calls. Lying in our bed, my head was spinning, and my mind was racing a mile a minute. I just wanted to scream till I lost my voice.

The kids came in the room, climbing in our bed and started asking questions. "They took James, huh Mom?"

Dijuan asked.

"Yes, they did."

"I knew it. We saw them this morning. Is he coming home soon?"

"Jesus, no."

Dijuan had put a movie on and we all stretched out on the bed.

Kianne drifted off to sleep moments later.

***

Waking up to an empty bed was going to be devastating. Kianne turned toward the mirror that stood in front of James' side of the bed. She stared at her reflection, not sure what her plans were for the day. She called her mom and explained in very little detail what had happened and asked her to get there immediately. As soon as she hung up, the phone rang, It was James. After the automated lady finished talking, James softly spoke. "I love you." Kianne begin to cry instantly.

"Hey, everything will be okay."

"I hope youre right."

"I am. You have to trust me. Besides I truly think you should keep the store. You never know what might kick off."

"That means I have to be around your family. *Hell no*, James. I'm moving where I feel comfortable."

"Okay Bae, it's your call. But babe, I do need you to do one thing. I know it may be hard, but I truly need you to call the numbers under Nia and Sha and see if they are ok. Can you do that?"

"James must have been smoking when he got picked up. This nigga just really asked if I could call his ex-bitches? I didn't give a fuck about them nor their wellbeing." Kianne took a deep breath and exhaled. Rolling her eyes with a smile plastered on her face—sure. It was only because she could rub in their faces that he married her.

"Thanks, love!" Then James went on to explain what happened in the investigation room. They told him they had been watching him for a while now and showed him pictures of people he never saw. Kianne sat shaking her head. All this was crazy. Their twenty minutes flew by fast and before they knew it, the call was over.

James wanted Kianne to stay in Monroe for whatever reason. Now he knew she couldn't stand it down here.

Besides his family not liking her— she didn't trust his family any more than she trusted herself in a Gucci store with his credit card. Where he would get the idea that she would stay was beyond her. If the store were to make enough to pay the house note, house bills and cover the store while he was gone— then maybe she would have considered it or even considered keeping the store open and checking on it monthly. Kianne would have to be in the situation where she was able to fly back and forth. And that wasn't the case now. They were on a straight budget and she had to get a nine to five to stay on top.

Kianne started to go through James' phone as requested. Looking for those bitches numbers. With clenched teeth, she dialed Sha's first. A perky voice answered, "Hello." She must have thought it was my husband she wanted so badly calling. With a grin that matched the Grinch, Kianne recited, "Hey this is James' WIFFFFFFFFE Kianne. He got picked up and he asked me to check on you and make sure you didn't get arrested too." If only I could see her face when she heard "wife." With a smile Kianne listened. *"I'm good."* Click. The bich hung up. Good, because I didn't care if the hoe went back to jail or not. All right, Nia...Kianne hit talk, and it went to voice mail. She called again. A deep voice answered, "Hey you!"

"Yeah, this is James' WIFFFFFE Kianne. James got arrested and he asked me to call and make sure you were good." The phone went silent.

"Hello?"

"Yeah, I'm good," and she hung up.

After all that had happened today, Kianne was in the best mood she has ever been in since their move to Monroe. She made a few more calls. Their ship was sinking and people were trying to get all they could before they drowned. Nigga's that owed James money was ignoring Kianne calls. A few said they gave money to Karen. But she denied ever receiving anything. Since the Feds took her credit cards, she tried James' accountant—there was no answer. She then called Enterprise to set up a ride for pick-up Kianne was not having his mom and dad drive her around to be all in their business. By the time she was dress, Enterprise was outside. Allowing the boys to stay home from school—she told them she was leaving.

Once Kianne obtained a rental, she headed to the store to pack. Mr. Hill, the owner of the build wife just happened to stop by. Trying to get Kianne to stay. She called her husband as if she was telling on her. Kiane explain she had no intentions of staying.

One by one James family members popped up at the store. While Kianne was in the office, Karen peaked in asking about a cell phone James promised for their anniversary. All Kianne seen was hands out. The only words they spoke was "Give me, give me." She laughed to herself— because she saw it coming and was pretty sure she told James. Everybody around them was stealing. Dre dirty ass was taking his off the top from the very beginning. I just wish he had consulted with me before he made any decisions.

Kianne finished packing the store up. She called her stepson and god-son to come down to help move. After finding out that one of the guys who tried to rob him was suppose to be a family members, she was anxious to leave Monroe.

Needing the help but not wanting it. Kianne accepted her mother-in-law, sister-in-law and the kids help to pack the house up. As for his mother, she only came to be nosey. Joe seemed so innocent but was ran by that woman. Kianne just wanted to get as far away from them as possible. Once Ray and Maliq made it, the house was basically packed, and the truck was almost loaded.

Once they finished loading the truck it was dark. Placing a padlock on the back—she left the truck at the house, then headed to stay at a hotel. Ever since the shooting Kianne nerves were bad. She stopped sharing information on her whereabouts.. Finding a hotel in West Monroe, Kianne grabbed two rooms and got in the bed. Anxious to leave that hell hole, she drifted peacefully to sleep.

The sun beamed through the curtains, Kianne rolled over and looked at her phone. It was 9 am—Kianne wanted to be on the road immediately. She texted the boys to get up. After eating breakfast, they headed over to the house and placed the Cadillac on the trailer. Karen and Joe met them at the house then followed them to the gas station. Once the truck and the van were filled up, they said their goodbyes. Pulling off, driving down Forsythe heading east, glancing in the mirror, Kianne watched Joe hold Karen in his arms as she shed tears—as if she really cared that they were leaving. Kianne smiled a beam of joy. She never wanted to see Monroe again.

~On the Move~

Kianne hadn't planned the move back to Minnesota very well, by the time they made it into Tennessee the starter went out on the van Ray was driving. Thankful for full coverage, Geico sent one of their partner towing companies to come pick up the truck and tow it to the nearest shop. Kianne and the boys found a hotel and called it a night.

Watching the morning news and with the storms coming into Kansas, she was pushing their luck. The shop managed to get the truck fixed before noon and they were back on the road. Running from the storms and twenty hours later, they all drove into Richfield, MN. Pulling into the La Quinta Inn off Highway 494 and Nicollet Avenue. No one knew Kianne and the family was coming back besides family.

As they got checked in, the boys passed out in their

room—but of course, Kianne had to get to work and look for housing. Living in hotels was not an option. Kianne made a few of calls and left messages on a couple of houses she found on Craigslist. As well as calling James' old landlord to see if that house was still available. Just like expected, Savon left it astray. What a friend. As the sun began to rise Kianne got in the shower and crawled in the bed. Knowing the little one was glad she was resting her body. Kianne dozed off into the greatest sleep since James was arrested.

***

For seven days Kianne fasted and prayed that things would get better. Speaking with her Pastor on several occasions on the trauma that she was dealing with. Living by faith and refused to ask family for help. Finding housing was difficult; it was a week before she found a permanent place to live. And it wasn't long before news broke loose that she was back in town.

During the happy days of her life, there was not one person she could call a friend that showed their genuine concern. People's true colors started to show. Despite the many questions that were asked, not once was she asked about her emotional wellbeing. Pregnant under extreme stress, and they were more worried about her husband's situation and if she was leaving him. Kianne got a call from a person she thought was a friend for many years. At this moment she finally accepted the fact that they weren't.

"Girl, why didn't you call me? I thought we were better than that! I heard at the barbershop! What happened? Did he leave you with money? Are you going to leave him? Why didn't you tell me your husband was in jail?" she blurted out. "Is that why you moved back to Minnesota?"

"It's not up for conversation; in fact, none of my business is."

"Well, when you're ready to talk, call me."

As if that's what Kianne wanted to do—pick up the phone and cry on her shoulder so she could run and tell her business like she did her other so-called friends. *Girl, bye*, Kianne laughed. Kianne found out about who was stepping out on their man with a woman and within their circle. Half the females she never met, and it was more than she cared for. So, Kianne could only imagine what had already been said about her.

Driving down 35W South, heading to get her job back at Serenity Beauty Salon. Having the option to not work, she chose otherwise.

~Plea Bargain~

It had been almost a year since James was arrested, although it felt so much longer. Kianne was just getting back to a normal routine in life. Pulling into the parking lot of Fantastic Sam's on 66th and Nicollet Avenue south. Like always, she was running late for work. Reaching in the back seat of her Cadillac to get her bags. Kianne phone rang and their attorney's name flashed on the screen. Whenever he called, she would begin to panic. Kianne's voice cracked as she answered. He called about a deal the Feds had on the table and that she needed to get James to accept what was being offered to him: 12 years and 7 months to 17 ½ years. *"Could I really do this amount of time? Them a lot of damn years."* With all the lies between the Feds and the niggas that snitched —it was better than 20 to life as the papers were showing in the beginning. Knowing her husband, he wasn't going for any of it. It was going to be hard explaining to this man that taking what they were offering him was best. Kianne just wanted him home as soon as possible. Putting her thoughts aside, Kianne went inside the salon. With four people waiting, she clocked in and got to work.

***

Eight hours later Kianne was heading home from work. James making his nightly call—*"You have a collect call from JAMES FIELDS, an inmate at Sherburne county jail. To accept this call dial 5 now."*

"Hey Bae."

"Hey Love, the lawyer called me today."

"Really? What he say?"

"He told me they put a deal on the table and he will be out there soon to get you the paperwork. He said you're at a level 33, which puts you at one hundred and fifty months to two hundred-and ten months."

"What about the two point enhancement?"

"That still stands. Jase said he worked for you." Kianne could hear James' deep breathing. She could imagine his nose flaring up and his eyes closing in, something that he did when he was beyond livid.

"Babe, I need you to pull his paperwork, so I can see exactly what he told those people."

"Ok, I'll get it tomorrow."

"Well, enough about that. How's the boys?"

"Getting on my nerves, still fighting and going at each other. Damir still ain't trying to walk."

"They're boys—they will fight. Tell that boy to get it together. Well love—I want to keep the calls short, so we can have phone time throughout the month. I love you and will talk to you tomorrow."

"Ok love, talk to you tonight." Kianne knew James was upset. She heard it in his voice. It was frustrating when you thought you had some real niggas in your corner, then come to find out that the ones closest to you are the ones to turn on you. It killed Kianne to see him in this situation and she couldn't do anything about it. Kianne sister told her Jase was going to run his mouth. That's what happened with his first federal case. Then he was going around telling folks James snitched. Everybody was serving time but his ass. Besides, after pulling his paper work- it was very clear. He words were, "I started helping Mr. Fields around December 2009 until July or October 2010." *But which one was it? October 2010 was when he was questioned.*

~Sentencing~

I woke up stressed Tuesday morning February 2, 2012. I was up before the alarm went off. Lying in our bed, my thoughts were far and wide. I was scared, lost, hurt and excited. Today was the day that held our fate. It could be 20 years to life, and if we were blessed it could be less. I was wondering if he would get the same time as the others or no time at all.

Rolling out of the bed, I slid to my knees and said a morning prayer. That was all I did after James left—pray. They say you don't call on Him until you need him. At this point I became so in tune with the Lord. He was the only one I could rely on, trust and give all my pain to. At times I didn't know whether I was coming or going. I gathered the kids and headed to court.

Leaving the house, we made a pit stop at McDonalds. I don't think the boys understood what was happening; the drive was long and quiet. Joe called me to see if I had made it yet. I had just parked and was coming up in the elevator. Joe tried to explain what would happen, but I was not sure if I heard everything. I just gave him a blank stare.

As we went to sit in the courtroom, they brought James in like he was a violent animal. The look on his face showed a glimpse of happiness seeing the kids and me. As his eyes scanned the room and made their way toward our attorney, that happiness disappeared. That man told so many lies and gave such great hope. We both just knew he was coming home, due to the attorney who was supposed to be in the legal world. James realized Joe was selling him for financial gain.

He looked back and smiled, waved at the boys and blew me a kiss. I could tell it was killing him inside, knowing he was moments away from being taken away from his family for a longer period of time. The thought of the time we were facing pierced in his black beady eyes. It was amazing how the system could use the words of one criminal to bring another to court and give them time with no evidence.

After a while the seats started to fill in with officer's faces I had seen before. His kids came in along with other family member's. He had a good support system within the courtroom, although it wouldn't make a difference in how the courts sentenced him.

"All rise," the deputy roared.

As the Judge sat down, he greeted everyone. "Good morning. Please be seated. We are here today in the case of United States of America versus James Earl Fields. If I could have the attorneys make their appearances, please."

My stomach was in knots; my mouth was dry. I was so anxious. One of the DAs I remembered from our Vegas trip stood up. "Good morning, Your Honor. Andrew Winters, LeeAnn Bell, and James Alexander appearing on behalf of the United States," Winter stated.

"Good morning, Your Honor. Joe Friedberg for Mr. Fields, who is present."

Joe seemed so calm, but then again he did this for a living.

"Good morning to both of you," the Judge replied. "Mr. Fields previously pled guilty to conspiracy to distribute and possession with intent to distribute cocaine. So the government has received a copy of the PSI, correct?"

"Yes, Your Honor," Winters stated.

"All right. The parties initially disputed the amount of cocaine for which Mr. Fields should be held responsible, as well as the role he played in the offense. I plan to take everything I hear from both parties into consideration," the Judge stated nonchalantly

As I sat and listened, this wasn't what I expected or how I expected it to go. The judge kept going on about James' role, what he made and spent, as if they knew. I took a deep breath as the judge continued on about James' past.

"In sum, during your entire life, Mr. Fields, you have either committed crimes or have been in prison. I do not believe that this Criminal History Category of III substantially over-represents the seriousness of your criminal history or the likelihood that you will commit other crimes. Therefore your motion for a departure under Section 4A1.3B is denied."

"Your Honor, if one steps back and look at this case, I

believe there were seven defendants in this conspiracy, or conspiracy that was alleged originally, and if you step back and look at it, Mr. Fields is not really one bit different than the rest of them. He's not any better, and he's not any worse. By the time he got involved in this case, there really was nobody for him to cooperate against him because everybody had cooperated against him—even if he wanted to, Your Honor. This case was set up and fixed. Mr. Fields was added to this case after every other defendant was charged and took their deals. In all honesty, the government did not know who Mr. Fields was until the defendants took their pleas. If everyone had just pled guilty and allowed the court to take its course, he would not be here."

The Judge stared at Joe like his ass was on backwards. I could tell the Judge did not care about anything Joe had to say. I was worried. All the praying, and the small glimpse of hope I had, was washed away by his hardened stare.

Joe continued, "There isn't any violence involved. There is a group of people who were doing this together but independently. The leadership roles are really not there. Everybody did pretty much what they wanted to do. I know that when you look at Mr. Fields' record, it admittedly looks terrible, but this is a guy that at least made an attempt at living a law-abiding life when he got out. Whether or not he would have kept working when the company went on strike or the employees went on strike is an open question, but he made a try at it. I don't see Mr. Fields as being one bit different than the other people involved in this case, and his sentence ought to be somewhere between one hundred twenty months and one hundred fifty months."

"Thank you, Mr. Friedberg."

"Mr. Fields, if you want to say anything on your behalf this morning..."

"Yes thank you, Your Honor, for giving me a chance to address the court."

James openly apologized to the children and myself, and to all the family that was present. He openly expressed how no one worked for him, but with him, that every man was for himself. He didn't make anyone do anything they did not want to do.

"All right," the judge cut James off. "I will ask for the two of you to have a seat so that I can hear from Mr. Winters. Mr. Winters, please approach."

"Thank you, Your Honor. As we've stated in our position paper, we believe a sentence within the guidelines range is appropriate. We have referenced 180 months, which is fair due to the crimes that have been committed. Your Honor, we are seeking the full amount. Thank you."

"Ok Mr. Fields, if I could please have you back at the podium for sentencing…" The Judge spoke with his head in the papers he was signing off on.

I shifted on the bench, my hands started to sweat and I became fidgety.

"I have carefully reviewed the presentence investigation report and the addendum to the report. I have also read a letter that I received this morning from Mr. Fields. I now accept the plea agreement, and I am prepared to impose the sentence."

I looked back at the kids. My sister Felicia was here. "It is the judgment of the Court that you, James Earl Fields Jr., are sentenced to prison for a term of 180 months. No fine is imposed. No restitution is ordered. You must pay a special assessment in the amount of one hundred dollars to the United States, due immediately."

You could hear a pin drop. I stared at the Judge with hatred in my heart. Burning water ran down my cheeks; my heart felt as if it was in throat; I couldn't breathe. I looked back at the children in the pew behind me, and then looked at our six-month-old baby. He had no idea what was going on around him. The other family members gasped for air; their hard breathing and movement filled the room. Winters leaned back in his chair with a grin, as if he had won a million bucks. On the right side of the courtroom, the other officers smiled, giving silent fist shakes as they mouthed, "Yes". The hard stare on my face showed my anger but I refused to break down in front of these folks. The judge stood up to exit through the side door, and the marshals grabbed James to escort him out. We locked eyes; his anger and my pain danced in the middle of the courtroom. The moment I blinked, he was gone.

Exiting the courtroom, I sat on a bench just outside the doors. I was in a daze. The children and some other family members lingered as well. I couldn't think. I wanted to cry but tears wouldn't escape my eyes. My sister called my job to let them know I wasn't coming in.

I drove home in silence. The boys were just as quiet. Damir made spit bubbles in his car seat. After getting food, we pulled into the driveway of our house. As the boys entered the house, I exhaled as I broke down. The tears started to flow. My life had changed from good to horrible. We had a whole year of togetherness. I was lost mentally and emotionally. I attended church weekly. I fast and prayed day in and out. I felt my prayers weren't getting answered when I wanted them. The years would pass, I knew the laws would change and the time would decrease. But I felt I needed to do something.

Through the sobs and tears, wondering if I was doing the right thing. Standing by my husband's side. So many theories running through my head. Is it worth it? The long drives, the searches, being hassled by police. Willing to give anything in this world to fix this situation and bring my babe home. I would surely tell on every nigga that grinned in my face, flashing their money. Setting up the ones who turn their backs on him. Put matters in my own hands. But the fact was the law won, family burnt us, and I was again alone with not two but three young boys to raise. Fifth-teen years is a long time; I was starting all over again. My purpose of finding a father for my boys—a man I could love and who loves me; was now on hold. All James and I had was prayer and faith. Besides his ex-bitch constantly harassing me through social media and my obnoxious partying behavior.

We managed to run this course yet together. And as every married couple, we have our issues, yet we continue to pray together. I praise God that this bid is almost over. 2019 is finally here!

ABOUT THE AUTHOR

Kimberly Fields is an author who was born in Minneapolis and grew up in Saint Paul. She attended Century College in Minnesota and attained qualifications in AAS Criminal Justice and Cosmetology. Since then she has worked for the US Bank and for herself. She still lives in Saint Paul today, with her husband and three boys.

She has been a keen writer for as long as she can remember and has been a prolific blogger in the past, writing for many diverse blogs. But it is writing novels that Kimberley enjoys the most and her books **KASH** and **A Woman's Reality** are both available through her website.

In her free time, Kimberley likes to sew and is a keen reader, with Eric J. Dickey and Zane and Nikki Turner books being among her favorites. She also enjoys anything to do with arts and crafts, cooking and baking and loves to travel when the opportunity arises.

In the future Kimberley would love to be able to write full time and become someone's favorite author, sharing as many of the stories she has in her head with as wide an audience as possible.

You can contact Kimberley Fields or see what she is writing about next at:

Website: www.kimberlyafields.com